London

ARCHITECTURAL ASSOCIATION

A guide to recent architecture

...

Samantha Hardingham

London

A guide to recent architecture

• • • ellipsis KÖNEMANN

•••

London: a guide to recent architecture

CREATED, EDITED AND DESIGNED BY
Ellipsis London Limited
55 Charlotte Road London EC2A 3QT
E MAIL ...@ellipsis.co.uk
www http://www.ellipsis.co.uk/ellipsis
PUBLISHED IN THE UK AND AFRICA BY
Ellipsis London Limited
SERIES EDITOR Tom Neville
SERIES DESIGN Jonathan Moberly
LAYOUT Pauline Harrison

COPYRIGHT © 1996 Könemann
Verlagsgesellschaft mbH
Bonner Str. 126, D-50968 Köln
PRODUCTION MANAGER Detlev Schaper
PRINTING AND BINDING Sing Cheong
Printing Ltd
Printed in Hong Kong

ISBN 3 89508 281 3 (Könemann)
ISBN 1 899858 08 3 (Ellipsis)

Samantha Hardingham 1995

Contents

Introduction

Now in its third edition, this book still contains descriptions of more than 100 built projects which represent the way London has evolved since 1980, but the contents of each edition have evolved. Projects that have proved to have short life-spans have been put aside to make way for new buildings and updates on strategic developments. The aim has been to keep the guide as up-to-date as possible – in this case a line has been drawn at, roughly, spring 1995.

The aim of the guide is to initiate an architectural tour of London, pointing out some of the latest building types and techniques on the way. Although projects are discussed individually, it is important to view each one in the larger context of the city. The gaps will be filled in by your own observations.

Understanding why London looks the way it does today depends on a basic knowledge of the country's politics. Britain has been in the hands of a Conservative government for 16 years. In the early 1980s, Prime Minister Thatcher initiated the deregulation of the public services that form the essential infrastructure of the country. The lifting of state control was intended to promote competition and, as a result, to result in better services. Refuse collection, telecommunications, water, gas, electricity, and bus services are just some examples of utilities that have been wholly or partially privatised. Responsibility has been relocated from the state or local government to individual companies – if they become negligent or even insolvent then the service deteriorates.

In 1986 the Labour-run Greater London Council was abolished. The only voice which could speak for the whole city was replaced by numerous bodies with special areas of interest, with the leftovers mopped up by the London Residuary Body. The result is a lack of coordination and a failure to set standards for the fundamental services that make up the city's infrastructure – there is no unified plan.

The effects on building are diverse. On the one hand there is a dearth of council housing. As council tenants were encouraged to buy their homes, the Government failed (and still fails) to replenish the housing stock. At the same time we have witnessed a building boom. This was concentrated in the City of London (the financial centre) and the under-developed Docklands where British and North American developers took the opportunity to build vast amounts of office space (providing all the services necessary for computerised trading) and luxury housing to accommodate well-paid employees. Concrete- or steel-framed buildings with granite cladding, sporting pop-classical motifs, were quick to build and provided an instantly grandiose façade for any company. Few of these speculative buildings could be listed as examples of a distinguished architecture (and most of the properties remain unlet since the economy began to decline in 1989), but they are collectively a social, economic and architectural phenomenon. Battersea Power Station (built by Sir Giles Gilbert Scott in 1929–1935) is another victim of the get-rich-quick philosophy. Margaret Thatcher inaugurated the scheme to gut this unique landmark and convert it to a theme park, but predictably money ran out and now the building lies crumbling like a decaying dinosaur. Its cousin, Bankside Power Station, is about to undergo plastic surgery and will reemerge as a Museum of Modern Art, designed by the Swiss architects Herzog & de Meuron.

Key events which initiated some architectural discussion in the early and mid 1980s include the Prince of Wales's debut on the architectural stage at Hampton Court, when he invited the public to participate in a Classicism *versus* Modernism debate. The Prince seemed certain that living in a Palladian-style *cul-de-sac* and shopping in a Tudoresque super-

London: a guide to recent architecture

market would preserve the essential qualities of the British Isles whilst protecting us from the vile threat of modernisation. The scheme to redevelop Paternoster Square and Peter Palumbo's proposals for the Mappin & Webb building in the City were both at the centre of these kinds of debates. Max Hutchinson, president of the Royal Institute of British Architects at the time, retaliated in a book entitled *The Prince of Wales: Right or Wrong? An Architect Replies* (Faber & Faber 1989). A decade on, these conversations have filtered through to the regions, enabling cities to embrace a new generation of ideas.

The launch of the National Lottery in 1994 is set to make a tremendous impact on building in London. Funds from the scheme are fed into four departments: the Department of National Heritage, the Arts Council Lottery Fund, the Sports Council, and the Millenium Commission – all of these are receiving proposals for new schemes. For instance, a feasibility study for Sir Richard Rogers' proposal to enclose the South Bank in a glass tent is being funded by the Arts Council. The Millenium Commission is to be disbanded soon after 2001, so it is looking to fund an immediate surge of projects.

Other promising recent developments can be found in schemes addressing the city's infrastructure: the extension of the Docklands Light Railway, the opening of the Limehouse Link which has improved access to Canary Wharf, and the long-delayed approval of the Jubilee Line extension. This will have stations designed by the likes of Foster Associates, Alsop & Störmer, Michael Hopkins & Partners, and Troughton McAslan, and is due for completion in 1998.

Many practices, large and small, are now designing smaller, quick-build schemes, often with challenging briefs and budgets, producing an enormous variety of projects and expanding the conventional architectural vocabulary. Examples include Allies and Morrison's Entertainment Pavilion at the Hayward Gallery and the Heathrow Airport Visitors' Centre by Bennetts Associates.

Under the plethora of speculative office developments, countless shop refurbishments and a distinct dshortage of public housing, trademarks of the 1980s, a very diverse range of building types has emerged in London in the 1990s. Nicholas Grimshaw's Waterloo International Terminal – a major engineering feat – provides an architectural landmark for London as the city approaches the millenium. But at the same time the completion of a wholly modern private house, designed by Future Systems and built in a conservation area, illustrates how we are growing more accustomed to change and new ideas springing up in our backyards too.

Acknowledgements

Thank you to all the architects for keeping me up to date with their work, to Paul Finch for providing up-to-the-minute, funny yet newsworthy building bulletins, to Tom Neville for working so hard to enable the project to continue for another year, and above all to Willy McLean who since the last edition has become my fantastic and supportive husband.

SH May 1995

Using this book

The guide is divided into 13 sections. Each section defines an area of London where there are buildings of interest. Most can be covered on foot. Transport details are listed under each entry. The map coordinates for the standard edition of the *AZ London Street Atlas* are also listed under each entry after the address to guide you to the precise location of a building.

If you wish to read more about any of the buildings, the architects or this particular era I suggest a visit to the library at the Royal Institute of British Architects, Portland Place, London W1 (check opening hours and the fee situation before you go). All the periodicals here are well catalogued and there are special files on major projects such as the hugely controversial British Library.

London: a guide to recent architecture

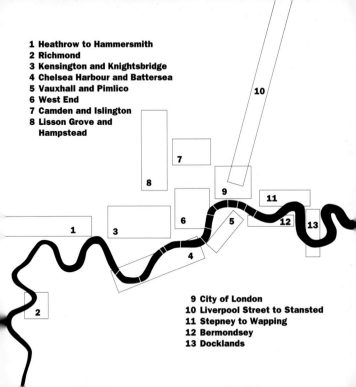

1 Heathrow to Hammersmith
2 Richmond
3 Kensington and Knightsbridge
4 Chelsea Harbour and Battersea
5 Vauxhall and Pimlico
6 West End
7 Camden and Islington
8 Lisson Grove and Hampstead

9 City of London
10 Liverpool Street to Stansted
11 Stepney to Wapping
12 Bermondsey
13 Docklands

Heathrow to Hammersmith

Heathrow Airport Visitors' Centre

The Visitors' Centre provides a permanent location for an exhibition which describes how the airport works, promoting the benefits as well as addressing the environmental issues which are raised by the airport's operation. It is both a centre for information (a model of the proposed Terminal 5 project by Richard Rogers is on display) and a new home for the local job centre, serving as a complaints box while locating the building positively in the community.

The building is made up of two walls which sandwich the main exhibition hall. The north-facing screen wall, clad in steel mesh, extends along the full 100-metre length of the site to separate the exhibition hall from the busy A4 Bath Road. In contrast, the south wall is a thin, transparent box made from a structural steel frame clad in frameless glass. This area accommodates service and access walkways made from galvanised steel grillage (doubling up as solar shading for the interior space). The café on the mezzanine level offers a panoramic view through the south wall of aircraft taking off and landing and acts as an acoustic barrier. The simplicity of structure and the clarity of the purpose of this small building creates a model on which airports themselves should be built.

ADDRESS Newell Road, Hounslow, Middlesex
CLIENT Heathrow Airport Limited
CONTRACT VALUE £3 million
SIZE 18,060 square metres
BY ROAD follow the A4 Great West Road out of Hammersmith. This becomes the Bath Road. Pass the Visitors' Centre on your left, take the next turning left after the Ramada Hotel and follow signs
ACCESS open Tuesday to Friday 10.00–19.00; Saturday 10.00–17.00

Heathrow to Hammersmith

Bennetts Associates 1995

Bennetts Associates 1995

Hilton Hotel

The hotel adopts the scale of the nearby hangars. It comprises 397 identical bedrooms, each with prefabricated bathroom, stacked either side of an atrium which is cut diagonally at each end to form a parallelogram in plan.

There are three elements to the construction. Originally the rooms were to be entirely prefabricated, stacked up and concrete poured between them. A nice idea, but time was short so reinforced-concrete slabs were cast *in situ* with acoustic insulation between cement particle board as wall partitions. The atrium is a separate steel-frame structure of round columns and lattice trusses. This whole structure is wrapped within a single-layer weathering membrane on the roof and white fibre-cement panels (Pyroc) on the exterior walls. They form a rainscreen and although economical are already acting as a pollution gauge, turning grey around the edges. The metal-look panels are continued inside on the interior walls of the atrium where the panels roughly meet the steel framework.

The finer detailing is in the glass curtain walls at each end of the atrium. Two layers of toughened glass are bolted either side of steel latticework to frame a considerable view of the terminal to the west and the approach road and landing 'planes to the east.

The atrium, which could accommodate 250 double-decker buses, is naturally flooded with light. 'Dancers 1990' by Alan Jones slices through the lofty space – the intention is good but perhaps the suspended wing of a jumbo jet would have given a better sense of scale and place. The internal courtyard is cluttered with restaurants, bars and seating areas decked out in rather unfortunate patterned carpets, light fittings and canvas canopies. These misplaced touches turn the building into yet another container rather than a rigorous piece of architecture.

Manser Associates 1990

Manser Associates 1990

Single rooms have a view of the atrium activities, in case one is feeling lonely, and double rooms are on the outside with a view of the docked Concorde on the north side. Each room is excessively upholstered and double-glazed for acoustic insulation – as a result they are quiet but cramped and claustrophobic. Perhaps this is a ploy to encourage guests to spend more time in the livelier atmosphere of the atrium and fill the many leather sofas.

I suggest hitch-hiking or catching a ride in the hotel buggy to get to the terminal rather than taking the endless and disorientating trek along the enclosed bridge link – sub-zero temperatures in winter.

ADDRESS Terminal 4, Heathrow, Middlesex
CLIENT BAA plc Hotel Development
STRUCTURAL ENGINEER YRM Anthony Hunt Associates
INTERIOR DESIGN Peter Glynn Smith Associates
TUBE Heathrow Terminal 4 – Piccadilly Line
ACCESS open

Manser Associates 1990

Stockley Park

Forty minutes' drive from central London, 20 minutes to the M25 and the rest of the UK, and five minutes by taxi to Heathrow Airport and the rest of the world. Stuart Lipton of Stanhope Properties plc led a master-plan in 1984 to clear up this 100-hectare site, which had been used as a dump for metropolitan rubbish since 1916, and transformed it into a new breed of business park. After a close study of the heavily polluted Grand Union Canal, which ran near to the site, and research into the toxicities in the soil, 3.5 million cubic metres of rubbish were ceremonially moved north to create a 'naturally' contoured landscape.

Lipton made sure that no expense was spared in making this the only place that large international companies would want to use as their UK headquarters. Land reclamation was carried out by a firm from the Netherlands, trees were brought in from Belgium, geese from Hawaii, Sir Norman Foster, Ian Ritchie, Troughton McAslan, Sir Richard Rogers, Eric Parry, Skidmore, Owings & Merrill, Inc., and Geoffrey Darke were commissioned to design buildings (all variations on the theme of a shell-and-core, two- or three-storey, steel-framed construction), and the Prince of Wales performed the opening ceremony.

The idea was to create a high-quality environment that could service nearby towns as well as the business community – social facilities include a nursery, immaculately landscaped gardens, a health club, golf course, bars and restaurants and a bus service which is linked to local schools. All that is needed to complete the picture is a uniform for all employees – a Star Trek outfit would be more appropriate here than a pin-stripe suit.

Arup Associates as masterplanners have designed more than 12 buildings on the site, providing adaptable space for a range of high-technology industries. They are designed as a series of pavilions with landscaped gardens immediately surrounding each one. In 1990 a total of 140,000

Arup Associates 1984–

Arup Associates 1984–

square metres of space was constructed. In particular, Arup's headquarters for Hasbro has won several awards.

Pavilions constructed to date at Stockley Park
A1.1, A1.2, A1.3, A2.1, A2.2, A2.3, A3.1, A3.2, B1 – Arup Associates
B2 (Apple Computers) – Troughton McAslan
b3 (BP) – Foster Associates
B4 (Apple Computers Phase II) – Troughton McAslan
B5 and B7 – Arup Associates
B6 – Geoffrey Darke
B8 – Ian Ritchie Architects
B9, B10 and B11 – Skidmore, Owings & Merrill, Inc.
B12 Eric Parry Associates
Arena Building (leisure complex) – Arup Associates

ADDRESS Heathrow, Middlesex
ENGINEER Ove Arup & Partners
LANDSCAPE DESIGN Bernard Ede and Charles Funke
BY ROAD leave M4 at junction 4, on to A408 (Stockley Road). Stockley Park is approximately 1.5 kilometres north
ACCESS the business park is open

Arup Associates 1984–

Arup Associates 1984–

The London Ark

As you cruise onto the Hammersmith flyover, the London Ark immediately communicates that this is not just any office block. The building readdresses the traditional form of the centrally governed business by creating a working community in which different companies can develop their own identity and contribute to the character of the common social environment contained within the central atrium – 'like a town under a roof'.

A significant step towards an ecologically sound office building, the Ark challenges the conventions of the building services which are often the cause of Sick Building Syndrome. The air-conditioning, for example, fixed to the ceiling, circulates a fresh-air supply through diffusers and across water-cooler batteries (set at 14°C to prevent condensation). The stale air is discharged through ventilators in the timber-lined atrium roof. Heating is a ceiling-mounted radiant system, using low-pressure hot water from a gas-fired boiler plant. Triple glazing reduces heat loss as well as shutting out traffic noise from the flyover. The 15,000 square metres of tiered, open-plan office space are flooded with natural light from the core. The intention is for information and air to flow freely around the building.

Bands of copper cladding, attached to the steel frame, appear to be protecting the delicate interior environment from the harsh exterior one, like a coat of armour. Although unpleasantly and overpoweringly brown at present, in time the copper will turn green. It is unfortunate that the clumsy brick supports will not undergo a similar, seemingly biological, transformation.

Ecologically sound inside maybe, but residents living in streets directly behind the Ark are now suffering the effects of noise from nearby underground trains rebounding off the curved side of the building and landing

Ralph Erskine 1991

Ralph Erskine 1991

in their back gardens. Erskine's response is to build a section of park over the exposed train lines, thereby deadening the noise and providing a new public space. Whether or not this actually materialises we shall have to wait and see.

It was hoped that the Ark would set a precedent for the development of environments for living, not just existing in, and that this would give rise to new building types rather than the acceptance of tarted-up old ones. There is still a lot of room for development; sadly, four years on, the Ark still remains unlet.

ADDRESS Talgarth Road, London W6 [5F 75]
CLIENT Ake Larson and Pronator
ASSOCIATED ARCHITECTS Lennart Bergstrom Architects and Rock Townsend Architects
PROJECT VALUE £33.5 million
TUBE Hammersmith – Piccadilly, District, Metropolitan Lines
BUS 9, 10, 27, 28, 31, 49, 391 to Hammersmith Broadway
ACCESS try telephoning Architectural Tours (081-341 1371) for an appointment

Ralph Erskine 1991

Ralph Erskine 1991

Thames Reach Housing and Thames Wharf Studios

This was once a Duckham's Oil depot, housed in two Edwardian brick warehouses with a 1950s' concrete block slung on the eastern end of the site. Rogers chose the 1950s' block for his own offices. The glass and steel-work was reconstructed but the essence of the building remains the same, i.e. the huge floor plates and the spectacular view across the river. There are windows on three sides of the building with the service core in the centre. The distinctive glass barrel-vaulted roof is a later addition, designed by Lifschutz Davidson Design.

The middle warehouse has been converted into workshop-type office spaces which are mainly occupied by designers and craftsmen. The River Café is on the ground floor, opening onto a garden terrace on the river front. The warehouse to the west has been turned into apartments. All the original load-bearing brick and blockwork remains the same, not an approach which is instantly associated with Rogers' previous high-tech record, but the white painted steel balconies, balustrades and walkways strapped onto each block are undoubtedly his.

The client played a prominent role in the design of the housing block, having a clear idea of the demands of the up-market residents being targeted. The dull interiors were contracted out to a more conventional interior designer. However, the river frontage is spectacular, with glazed curtain wall façades facing south west. Venetian blinds and natural through ventilation combat solar heat gain. The glass-brick tower which projects upwards from one of the blocks is part of John Young's private apartment (see page 32).

Rogers' theme is the creation of a community with shared public facilities and open-plan living and working space. His office is a community in its own right with the café and crèche for its employees. The lettable

Richard Rogers Partnership/Lifschutz Davidson Design 1984–1987

Richard Rogers Partnership/Lifschutz Davidson Design 1984–1987

space, occupied by design-orientated trades and industries, helps to fuel the working community and the opening up of another section of the riverside walk from Hammersmith to Putney Bridges adds to the public domain. The exercise here is in urbanism rather than architectonics.

Heathrow to Hammersmith

ADDRESS Rainville Road, London W6 [6E 74]
CLIENTS Housing: Croudace Construction; Studios: Marco Goldschied, Richard Rogers, John Young; Offices: H H Peggs; River Café: Richard and Ruth Rogers
STRUCTURAL ENGINEER Ove Arup & Partners/Hay Barry & Partners
CONTRACT VALUE £1034 per square metre
TUBE Hammersmith – Piccadilly, District Lines
BUS 9, 10, 27, 28, 31, 49, 391 to Hammersmith Broadway
ACCESS limited

Richard Rogers Partnership/Lifschutz Davidson Design 1984–1987

Heathrow to Hammersmith

Richard Rogers Partnership/Lifschutz Davidson Design 1984–1987

The Deckhouse

This private apartment, designed and owned by John Young, a partner in the Richard Rogers Partnership, is a complete exercise in industrial/nautical high-tech applied to a domestic situation. Every aspect of the apartment is obsessively thorough in its detailing, from the industrial coiled heating units on the wall to wire balustrades and gleaming stainless-steel fittings, each one a beautiful object in its own right. A south-facing, double-height glazed curtain wall exposes the living quarters (an open-plan dining/living room with a mezzanine bedroom level at the back) to the river, making the spectacular view a prominent part of the interior.

The bathroom tower is another spectacular *Blade Runner* feature and can be seen from the exterior poking up from the roofline. The focus is a sunken bath set in a polished screed floor in the centre of the round room. The walls are of glass brick and the ceiling is clear glass so light pours in from all around and there is a view of the heavens from the tub. Furnishings have been kept to a minimum, a few modernist chairs around a glass table. The building that has emerged is not necessarily new in terms of form (Pierre Chareau seems to have been a strong influence here), but the sum of the immaculate details and the hierarchy of rooms has created a total architecture.

ADDRESS 9 Thames Reach, Rainville Road, London W6 [6E 74]
CLIENT John Young and Marianne Just
STRUCTURAL ENGINEERS Hay Barry & Partners/Ove Arup & Partners
TUBE Hammersmith – Piccadilly, District Lines
BUS 9, 10, 27, 28, 31, 49, 391 to Hammersmith Broadway
ACCESS none

John Young 1991

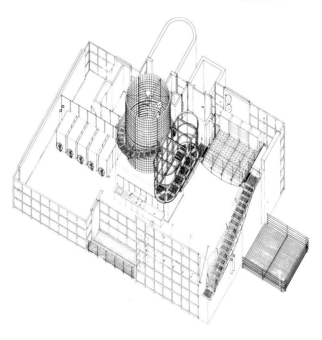

Heathrow to Hammersmith

John Young 1991

Richmond

Richmond Riverside

The site of this royally approved scheme is bound by the River Thames on the south side, Hill Street to the north, Bridge Street to the east, and the rest of Richmond village stretching out to the west. The brief was to provide 9900 square metres of office space, two restaurants, 28 flats and parking space for 135 cars. All this is disguised behind a Hollywood vision of old London town; convincing, but for the distinct lack of festive cheer about the place. Some of the original buildings still exist on the site, although they are hard to pick out … at first glance.

Face the scheme from across the river. On the left is a square block of two storeys, with arched windows and a roof surmounted by a cupola (the significance of this detail will become apparent in a moment). It is decorated with Doric and Ionic columns, drawing its jumble of references directly from Palladian villas, but here used as a restaurant. Behind this, running adjacent to the river, is the town hall called 'The Castle', built in 1873 by W J Ancell. Only the façade remains, looking like the leftovers of a Regency square. Next to it is the old town hall, now a public library, with a new French mansard roof (presumably added to increase floor space). Next along is the entirely new Hotham House, built in a patchy Georgian style which is given away by its genuine next-door neighbour, Heron House, built in 1716. Heron House has been fully restored and provides access through an archway into the new central square. The square is full of stucco buildings which are trying hard to pass themselves off as 100- to 200-year-olds when really they have not even reached their fifth birthday. The row is terminated by the prettier, Italianate Tower House, built in 1856 by Laxton. The Hill Street and Bridge Street façades are lined with arcades, each block defined by a different order.

All the new buildings are built of load-bearing brick and lime mortar with reinforced-concrete slab floors and Welsh slate roofs. The appro-

Richmond

Erith & Terry 1988

Erith & Terry 1988

priate accoutrements are on the outside but functions have changed. Chimneys sitting on party walls and decorative cupolas (here's the trick) now become essential as disguises for modern air vents and ducting. On entering any of the buildings you realise the full extent of the exercise in deception when you witness bog-standard 1960s'-style office interiors being jammed between the neo-Georgian/Palladian/Gothic-Venetian façades. Raised floors and suspended ceilings cut through the full height of windows, obtrusive both from the inside and outside. The architect, Quinlan Terry, is reported to be equally disappointed with the interiors but surely such a vital detail could have been accommodated within a less dogmatic plan.

His ideal is 'to return to the letter and spirit of the Classical world, a world that is characterised by order'. The nature of Classicism is truth and its purity of form, the nature of Classical orders are that they are structural rather than ornamental: inside and outside were one and the same thing. Modernism (Mr Terry has called the movement 'a sign of the fall from grace') has more in common with the style and nature of Classicism than this architect is prepared to admit. Richmond Riverside is the scheme that architects love to hate but its subliminality seems to go down well with the local residents.

ADDRESS Richmond, Surrey [2J 89]
CLIENT Haslemere Estates
CONTRACT VALUE £20 million
TUBE Richmond – District Line
BR Richmond
ACCESS open

Richmond

Erith & Terry 1988

Richmond

Erith & Terry 1988

The Knight House

The Knight House is one of a rare breed of modern private houses to be built in the 1980s. David Wild's own house in Camden is the other obvious example, Wild himself being a great admirer of Chipperfield's work. 'I believe that architecture should celebrate primary enjoyment and permanent phenomena – light, space, nature … Modernism enables the enjoyment of these elements', says Chipperfield. This house certainly embraces all of these by providing a minimal shell which becomes animated by a play of light, materials and views of nature.

The project was to design an extension to a house belonging to a photographer. Daylight was of the utmost importance, not only for the photographer's studio on the first floor of the house, but also for all the interior spaces. A long extension, incorporating a new entrance, dark-room and living room on the ground floor and studio upstairs, formed an L-shaped house in plan. The pitched roof of the old building was levelled to make a flat roof terrace. Bedrooms upstairs and kitchen and dining room downstairs are accommodated in this revamped section of the house.

To make a complete rectangular plan, a wooden decked courtyard fills a corner on the ground level, framed by a concrete arch. This in turn frames the birch trees planted beyond, also reading as the edge of the building.

The street frontage, facing east, gives little away about the activities within. The architect designed it so that when the clients entered their home they would be in a tranquil world of their own. Views are directed towards the back of the house onto the garden and pond at the end of the living room. The simple spaces inside are not vast but they have been expanded by admitting as much natural light as possible and by the contrasting use of materials, textures and colours inside. Floors are oak,

David Chipperfield Architects 1987

Richmond

David Chipperfield Architects 1987

slate and terrazzo, changing according to the various activities in the house. Walls are concrete, some painted white and others left raw. The main staircase is made of flat steel. Each detail has been executed with fastidious restraint, a coolness that has been influenced by the architect's experience of working in Japan.

ADDRESS 16 Arlington Road, Petersham, Surrey TW10 9BY [D2 104]s
CLIENT Nick Knight
TUBE Richmond – District Line
BR Richmond
ACCESS none

Richmond

David Chipperfield Architects 1987

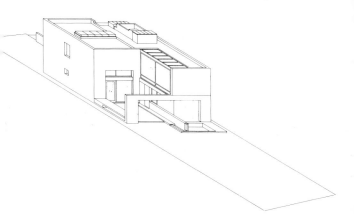

David Chipperfield Architects 1987

Kensington and Knightsbridge

Thames Water Ring Main Tower

A student competition was held to design a structure that would hide a surge pipe in the middle of the roundabout and at the same time celebrate the vast £250 million ring main project which now embraces central London. The winning entry was designed by students from the Royal College of Art who created this 15-metre-high barometer. The round tower is made of steel and glass (with the service ladder in the middle) and is animated by coloured water contained within the curved glass walls and spiraling its way up and down the tower to indicate the climatic extremes.

The adjacent classical shed is not related in any way to the winning design and is best ignored.

Kensington and Knightsbridge

ADDRESS Shepherd's Bush Roundabout, London W12 [F2 75]
CLIENT Thames Water
CONSULTANT ARCHITECT Alan Brooks Associates
STRUCTURAL ENGINEER Neil Thomas
TUBE Shepherd's Bush – Central Line
BUS 12, 49, 94, 295 to Shepherd's Bush Roundabout

Damien O'Sullivan and Tania Doufa 1994

Kensington and Knightsbridge

Damien O'Sullivan and Tania Doufa 1994

Westbourne Grove Public Lavatories

The project encompasses the whole of the triangular traffic island to incorporate landscape design as well as the design of the building itself. CZWG's unmistakeable approach comes into its own in this small but provocative urban folly. The three-sided plan has grown out of the shape of the site, the wide end accommodates the lavatories and attendant's kiosk and the pointed end of the triangle is a florist's kiosk. The pale aquamarine glazed brick walls sit on the pavement like a slice of delectable gateau, topped by a delicate glazed canopy roof with the clock stuck on the corner like a glacé cherry. Each feature is exploited to the full, even down to the stylised supergraphics on the lavatory doors to distinguish the GENTS from the LADIES.

There is no doubt that it is an improvement on its predecessors. It is unusually generous with space when so often minimum standard dimensions are applied for a facility of this type. A bold move by the local residents (the Pembridge Association actuallly promoted the idea of commissioning CZWG) to change the face of their neighbourhood.

ADDRESS junction of Colville Road and Westbourne Grove, London W11 [6H 59]
CLIENT The Royal Borough of Kensington and Chelsea Council Offices
STRUCTURAL ENGINEER Dewhurst MacFarlane & Partners
CONTRACT VALUE £190,000
SIZE site 700 square metres, building 60 square metres
TUBE Westbourne Grove – Hammersmith & City Line; Notting Hill Gate – Central, District and Circle Lines (both require a 5-minute walk to reach the site)
BUS 15, 23 to Westbourne Grove
ACCESS open

Kensington and Knightsbridge

CZWG Architects 1993

Kensington and Knightsbridge

CZWG Architects 1993

87 Lancaster Road

Steve Marshall describes this unusual commercial office block as an ode to Gerrit Rietveld's Schroeder House in Utrecht (1924). Obviously stylistically inspired by the clean lines of the Modern Movement, these young architects have experimented further with materials to make it stand out from the retro crowd. The roof structure is the specific feature which deserves attention. A floating, concave wing hovers over a 12-metre span, unsupported on columns. A stressed birch plywood box was used to achieve this slender canopy (steel would have been too deep) with Glulam beams imported from Sweden to form the shape. The plywood is strong but not stiff so the whole roof structure balances on steel hinges to allow for movement, and slopes towards the back to let water drain off.

The top-floor space is enclosed in 10 mm toughened glass in order to achieve the floating sensation. Slots are cut into the front and the back of the roof so that if the canopy should move on its hinges it will simply slide over the glass like a sleeve. The wood provides its own insulation and natural colour.

ADDRESS 87 Lancaster Road, London W11 [6G 59]
CLIENT Gladdings Estates & Developments plc
CONTRACT VALUE £1.45 million
SIZE 1140 square metres
TUBE Ladbroke Grove – Metropolitan Line
BUS 15, 52, 302 to Ladbroke Grove
ACCESS none

Munkenbeck and Marshall 1989–1991

Munkenbeck and Marshall 1989–1991

Ramesses II

This Sainsbury's Homebase diy store was the target of a colossal attack launched by architectural journalists in June 1987, when they asked the question, 'is this architecture, and if it isn't, then what is it?' In April 1987 Ian Pollard bought the site from British Rail and sold half of it to Sainsbury's. The deal included a design package for their store. The theme was Ancient Egypt, with a low-relief mural depicting Egyptian gods surrounding the vast single-storey shop, a car park fronted by a colonnade of Egyptian columns and an entrance marked by five Corinthian columns. All forms and colours were authentic, according to research carried out at the British Museum.

The package was constructed and everyone who passed by had a smile on their face. But … when an article came out in the *Architects' Journal* written by editor Peter Carolin, the alarm bells went off and Sir John Sainsbury ordered the immediate removal of the Corinthian columns and the colour from the colonnade. Carolin wrote: 'Architects must recognise the needs [Ian Pollard] seeks to satisfy but must find more attractive, appropriate and profound means of doing so. His buildings are advertising, not architecture.' I respect the *Architects' Journal* greatly but *really*, why is an Egyptian Sainsbury's any more a target for criticism than the more subversive mock-Tudor Tesco superstore? – the latter are springing up all over the country without embarrassment. Surely the commercial nature of the store suggests, precisely, a prime advertising opportunity.

ADDRESS Warwick Road, London w8 [4H 75]
CLIENT Sainsbury's Homebase
TUBE West Kensington – District Line
BUS 9, 10, 27, 28, 31, 49 to Warwick Road
ACCESS open

Peter Argyrou Associates on behalf of Ian Pollard 1988

Kensington and Knightsbridge

Peter Argyrou Associates on behalf of Ian Pollard 1988

Ecology Gallery, Natural History Museum

The gallery accommodates the new ecology exhibit in a chasm of Opti-white glass, illuminated with coloured lights to create the illusion of fire, water and a sheer glacial wall. Clear strips are cut into the walls, like rubbing the frost off windows, to reveal exhibits and parts of the existing building. Look out for literary quotes etched into the glass. Ribbed bellies of bridges traverse the corridor above your head to connect the different themes exhibited upstairs. Each bridge floor is made from a different material, evoking different aspects of the earth and its elements. These platforms allow you to pause and float in the space, to absorb your surroundings before you are drawn into the walls again to walk inside a leaf or be shovelled up by a giant digger.

Ritchie's environment is both interactive and reflective. Although some of the detailing is a bit flimsy the overall effect is informative and convincing.

ADDRESS Cromwell Road, London sw7 [4K 75]
CLIENT Natural History Museum
STRUCTURAL ENGINEER Ove Arup & Partners
CONTRACT VALUE £2 million
SIZE 3000 square metres
TUBE South Kensington – Piccadilly, Circle, District Lines
BUS 14, 74, C1 to Exhibition Road
ACCESS open

Ian Ritchie Architects 1991

Kensington and Knightsbridge

Dinosaur Gallery, Natural History Museum

This is a triumph of modernisation and preservation over mundane conservation. A new 84-metre raised walkway runs the full length of the Dinosaur Gallery in Alfred Waterhouse's elaborate Victorian neo-Gothic palace of natural science. The tensegrity structure's function is three-fold. In order to enhance the existing structure it holds services that illuminate the Victorian carvings of fish and animals on columns, treading lightly around these parts that previously went unnoticed. Secondly, it provides new circulation, views of the exhibits on the ground and close inspection of the old details. Thirdly, it forms a framework from which to hang dinosaur skeletons (a slight give in the cables causes them to twitch ominously).

Unfortunately, Imagination's temporary exhibition diplays do not correspond to possible views from the mezzanine. This lack of coherence should be rectified, but in the meantime you can enjoy the primary structure and its obvious spiny qualities.

ADDRESS Cromwell Road, London SW7 [4K 75]
CLIENT Natural History Museum
STRUCTURAL ENGINEER Ove Arup & Partners
TUBE South Kensington – Piccadilly, Circle, District Lines
BUS 14, 74, C1 to Exhibition Road
ACCESS open

Kensington and Knightsbridge

Herron Associates @ Imagination 1992

Wonders at the Natural History Museum

A modest work from an office which has received significant commissions in Germany and Tokyo. The museum has made an enlightened choice of architect in the past to regenerate interest. In this case, David Chipperfield was commissioned to redesign reception and admissions furniture and a display system for the permanent Wonders Exhibition in the bays of the main hall. The reception furniture has a characteristically Japanese horizontality: wooden slatted bases and sand-blasted glass screens which do not try to challenge the magnificence of the dinosaur skeleton in its grand Gothic abode (nor do they expose a new vision of the space as has Herron's intervention in the Dinosaur Gallery).

The two main issues for the exhibition to address were how to mediate between the monumental scale of the existing space and the small objects to be displayed, and how to accommodate the varying scale of the exhibits themselves in a unified way. Located in each bay is a uniform 4 x 4 metre primed steel wall. Each one has been customised to accommodate different objects by cutting out niches or adding shelves and plinths. The walls conceal all necessary lighting and monitor equipment, leaving a blank surface to show off the objects. Continuity is maintained between all the elements with the uniform shape and details in cast bronze, as found throughout the rest of the museum.

ADDRESS Cromwell Road, London SW7 [4K 75]
CLIENT Natural History Museum
TUBE South Kensington – Piccadilly, Circle, District Lines
BUS 14, 74, C1 to Exhibition Road
ACCESS open

Kensington and Knightsbridge

David Chipperfield Architects 1993

David Chipperfield Architects 1993

Issey Miyake

In the school of Chipperfield, Parry and Mather, Stanton Williams explore Modernist themes with more than a hint of traditional Japanese influence. The two philosophies work well together, producing pure spaces stripped bare to provide a natural and tranquil background for the few but stunningly sculptural garments. The large areas of empty space leave room for customers to wander around in, to adjust to the clothes and then to show them off.

The entrance of the shop simply acts as a display case and as a transitional space between the street and the inner sanctum of the shop. All the clothes are downstairs along one wall. The rest of the basement space is a stage set; a wall, a stair, a platform, all props for flaunting the wearable art works of Issey Miyake. As in David Chipperfield's shops for Equipment (see page 68), the natural colours of the materials provide the decoration – steel balustrading, oak floors, concrete walls – leaving the clothes to speak for themselves.

Stanton Williams's other retail projects in London include: Whistles, St Christopher's Place, W1 (1991); Hayward Gallery Bookshop, South Bank Centre (1991). They have also designed several exhibitions at the Victoria & Albert Museum, The Royal Academy of Arts and the Design Museum.

ADDRESS 270 Brompton Road, London sw3 [4c 76]
CLIENT Issey Miyake
CONTRACT VALUE £600,000 (for the design of three shops of similar scale and office/apartment)
TUBE South Kensington – Piccadilly, Circle, District Lines
BUS 14, 45A, 49, 249, 349 to Fulham Road and Sydney Street
ACCESS open

Stanton Williams 1990

Stanton Williams 1990

Michelin House

Michelin House is the Grade II listed original British headquarters of the Michelin Tyre Company. It has been restored and converted to accommodate the offices of the Paul Hamlyn Publishing Group, The Conran Shop and Oyster Bar and the Bibendum Restaurant.

The original construction is a reinforced-concrete frame, the first of its kind in England, designed by an untrained architect. Sixty steel columns have been threaded through the existing floors to support a new fourth floor without obstructing the main shop at ground level – a proposal of such complexity that it took 1300 separate drawings to detail it. Another new feature is the glazed wall on the Sloane Avenue façade which encloses the old loading bay, providing more shop space.

Original features have been lovingly restored, from the glass cupolas each side of the Brompton Road entrance and the stained-glass window of Bibendum to the tiles that run around what was the tyre-fitting bay and is now the stage for the lobster seller. Damaged tiles were patched with pigmented resin. It is fashionable to peruse the contents of the shop on Saturday mornings, buy an esoteric coal bucket from Bangalore, spot a design guru slurping oysters and then roam around the rest of Brompton Cross and identify other architect-designed shops.

ADDRESS Brompton Road, London SW3 [4C 76]
CLIENTS Paul Hamlyn and Sir Terence Conran
STRUCTURAL ENGINEER YRM Anthony Hunt Associates
CONTRACT VALUE £9 million
SIZE 36,500 square metres total
TUBE South Kensington – District, Circle, Piccadilly Lines
BUS 14, 45A, 49, 74, 249, 349, C1 to Fulham Road and Sydney Street
ACCESS open

Conran Roche (after François Espinasse, 1911) 1986–1987

Conran Roche (after François Espinasse, 1911) 1986–1987

Jigsaw

This is the grand salon of a chain of fashion shops which developed a new image for itself in association with Branson Coates Architecture from about 1988. Other branches are in Kensington High Street and St Christopher's Place. The Knightsbridge outlet is an appropriate tribute to an area well known as a superior shopping location.

Customers are lured in from the street by a huge organic, bronze column in front of a double-height glass façade. The ground floor, paved in stone, acts as an extension of the pavement. Green and grey make a mossy cove inside, then a sweeping terrazzo staircase carries you up into a glowing, carpeted main room. In the architect's own inimitably theatrical way, everything from the chromed mannequins and dripping blue-glass chandelier to the tongue chairs in brick-red velvet (for customers to lounge on) is sumptuous, reflecting the rich colours of the clothes themselves and the sheer joy of trying something on and showing it off. All these details were designed by the architects or Nigel Coates exclusively, with the mural designed and painted by Stewart Helm.

ADDRESS 31 Brompton Road, London SW3 [4C 76]
CLIENT Jigsaw Limited
STRUCTURAL ENGINEER Dewhurst McFarlane & Partners
TUBE Knightsbridge – Piccadilly Line
BUS 9, 10, 14, 19, 22, 52, 74, 137, 137A, C1 to Knightsbridge
ACCESS open

Branson Coates Architecture Limited 1991

Kensington and Knightsbridge

Branson Coates Architecture Limited 1991

Fifth Floor, Harvey Nichols

The foodies' wonderland, which is the Fifth Floor at Harvey Nichols, was born out of a brief to refurbish the top floor of the store. You emerge by escalator from the main store into a central marketplace, feeding onto an open café area, all covered by the partially existing 1970s' roof structure of triangular steel lattice beams covered by a pleated skin made up of acrylic diffusing panels and yellow-painted steel panels. The skin allows natural light to filter into the central area.

The north side accommodates a food hall which supplies everything edible and esoteric. The wine shop on the west side also acts as cellar to the bar and restaurant which are shielded from the main space by a glass screen, thus making them independently accessible after shop hours via elevators which connect directly with the street level.

Virtually all the furniture and fittings were designed or otherwise specified by Wickham & Associates: the café's plywood and MDF Pola chair to the cake stands with ball feet. Tthe detailing is on the bulky side, but the trademark is original and consistent throughout.

By capturing the activities of the street which enhance the life of so many European cities, and bringing them up to roof level, visitors can enjoy the decorative backdrop of the top of the Hyde Park Hotel and the Knightsbridge skyline rather than choke on the congested highway below.

ADDRESS Knightsbridge, London SW1 [2D 76]
STRUCTURAL ENGINEER Whitby & Bird
CONTRACT VALUE £5.4 million
SIZE 3000 square metres
TUBE Knightsbridge – Piccadilly Line
BUS 9, 10, 14, 19, 22, 52, 74, 137A, C1 to Knightsbridge
ACCESS open during licensed hours

Wickham & Associates 1992

Wickham & Associates 1992

Equipment

The product for this store is an elegantly folded silk shirt in a range of bold and beautiful colours. The whole shop acts as a display case for these shirts rather than individual shelving units in an anonymous space. The building materials have been selected for their neutrality and rawness so that they do not conflict with the strong product in any way, but help to enhance it, particularly in the way that light plays on the natural colours of the walls, floor and podium.

Chipperfield's approach to design is through composition rather than specific elements. He defines spaces with timber (an elm floor here), stone, concrete and stainless steel (in the shelves), letting these surfaces sculpt the quality of the interior.

There is another Equipment shop by Chipperfield on Brook Street, w1.

ADDRESS Sloane Street, London sw1 [3D 76]
CLIENT Equipment
TUBE Knightsbridge – Piccadilly Line
BUS 19, 22, 137, 137A, C1 to Sloane Street
ACCESS open

David Chipperfield Architects 1992

Kensington and Knightsbridge

David Chipperfield Architects 1992

Chelsea and Battersea

Chelsea Harbour

This site was a wasteland, used as a dump for crashed cars and toxic waste. Up until 1960 coal barges used to deliver their cargo to the London Underground Power Station on Lots Road. This unglamorous history did very little to help Ray Moxley of Moxley, Jenner and Partners convince anyone to back his idea that the site could become a high-class development. Finally, with backing from P&O and after having won a competition run by the British Rail Property Board (owner of the land), Moxley's dream came true, extremely quickly. Chelsea Harbour is thought to have been the fastest development of its size ever built in Europe. Planning permission was granted on 15 April 1986, the first piles were driven the next morning and twelve months later the first residents moved in.

The key elements of the scheme are the 75-berth yacht harbour, 439 luxury flats and 36 houses (occupied by film and rock stars) in various blocks arranged around squares, a five-star hotel, a shopping mall, office space, and underground parking for 1700 cars. Most of the buildings are four to six storeys high, apart from the Chelsea Crescent block on the river front which steps down from eight to five storeys, and the 20-storey Belvedere Tower (each flat occupies a whole floor), the landmark of the site, surmounted by a gold ball which goes up and down according to the level of the tide. Under the ground is a vast network of car-parking space. Ventilation is accommodated in the podia that raise all the flats above ground level by about a metre.

The key to the speed of the project lies in the way construction was organised. A fast-track method of building was adopted, meaning that design and construction went on simultaneously. To achieve an ambitious schedule, reinforced-concrete frames with flat slab floors were used throughout the site. Concrete allowed design flexibility, and when designs were being completed five minutes before work started on site the archi-

Moxley, Jenner and Partners 1986–1988

Moxley, Jenner and Partners 1986–1988

tects needed to leave as many options open as possible until the last moment. All the concrete conformed to one basic mixture so that if one area was not ready another would be, allowing the 600 cubic metres of concrete poured each day to be kept constant. Curtain walling, precast masonry and brickwork are used to clad the buildings. One of the more bizarre stories is that the local Civic Society complimented Mr Moxley on his 'sensitive restoration' of the buildings!

The atmosphere is somewhat bleak at Chelsea Harbour, particularly for an urban site. Evidence of any transport system connecting it to the rest of Chelsea is lacking and disturbing: cars are prohibited at ground level throughout the pedestrianised development; they are housed underground. As a result there are vast, empty paved areas between clumps of buildings. Restaurants and bars have been concentrated within the largely unlet Garden Market, isolated from living areas. Leaving the generic appearance aside, there is no coherence between any of the buildings and the facilities in the plan. The architect himself occupies one of the flats in the Belvedere Tower (from which he can view Plantation Wharf across the river, designed by his son) and is passionately optimistic about how the development will evolve in the future.

ADDRESS Lots Road, London SW10 [4A 76]
CLIENTS Chelsea Harbour Limited, a joint venture of the Peninsular and Orient Steam Navigation Company and Globe Investment Trust plc
CONSULTING ENGINEER Clarke Nicholls and Marcel
CONTRACT VALUE £150 million
SIZE total site covers 7.3 hectares
BUS C3 to Chelsea Harbour
ACCESS public spaces are open

Moxley, Jenner and Partners 1986–1988

Moxley, Jenner and Partners 1986–1988

Chelsea and Westminster Hospital

Following the closure of Westminster Hospital in Horseferry Road, this hospital embodies the Government's scheme to amalgamate many of London's hospitals, providing fewer beds for complex cases and leaving the rest to attend 'Super Health Centres' which I'm afraid don't actually exist yet (well, not in every community). Chelsea and Westminster Hospital provides 666 beds, clinical, research and teaching facilities, on-site accommodation for approximately 300 staff and medical students, a Mental Health Unit for 80 patients and facilities for 12 out-patients. It was commissioned and completed in a record 42 months.

With the exception of the rather heavy canopy designed by the engineers Atelier One, the brick and glass warehouse-look, five-storey front elevation (suggesting wide-span horizontal floors reaching from front to back) gives you no indication of what lies behind. The interior design focuses on a naturally ventilated central atrium, rising to seven storeys. It is covered by a pneumatic ETFE (ethylene tetra-fluorothylene) roof membrane, the largest expanse ever used to roof an atrium. The triple-layer foil membrane forms highly insulated cushions kept inflated by a constant stream of air fed through the extruded aluminium framework. The ground floor mall creates a semi-outdoor environment, providing seating/café areas, a pharmacy, crèche, hospital chapel and access to all departments in the building via three lift cores. The chapel is an independent structure within the atrium, emphasising the street-like quality of the space. Its stained-glass windows were transferred from the old Westminster Hospital.

There are three ante-atria each side of the central space forming light wells at the centre of the wards, and administrative offices which run around the perimeter of the building. The walls are lined with horizontal fins called Helmholtz resonators absorbing frequencies of sound which

Sheppard Robson Architects 1993

Chelsea and Battersea

Sheppard Robson Architects 1993

might build up throughout the vast internal spaces. The huge fins at the bottom of each well are part of the natural ventilation system: open in the summer, drawing in cool air from the outside. Heat generated from the perimeter rooms is used to heat the atrium in winter. At the rear of the building, housed in a two-storey basement there is a Combined Heat and Power Plant which generates electricity to power the hospital; excess power is sold on to the London Electricity Board, feeding into the city grid. Visual and physical links between all areas of the hospital have been created with uncovered walkways which traverse the central atrium.

The hospital has pioneered an impressive arts programme, with commissioned works by Alan Jones ('Acrobatic Dancer' – see Jones' work at the Hilton Hotel, Terminal 4, Heathrow), textiles by Sian Tucker, murals by Melvyn Chantrey, tapestry by Mary Fogg and a hanging by Patrick Heron. To my pleasant suprise the building did not have the usual disinfectant/boiled food aroma that impregnates so many hospitals – 'Catering' has wisely been located beyond the rear of the atrium. Before you get that far down the 116-metre-long space your breath has already been taken away by innumerable innovative features.

ADDRESS Fulham Road, London SW6 [2G 91]
CLIENT Riverside Health Authority
CONTRACT VALUE £177 million
SIZE 111,500 square metres
BUS 14, 211 to Fulham Road
ACCESS to the central atrium

Sheppard Robson Architects 1993

Chelsea and Battersea

Sheppard Robson Architects 1993

Riverside Offices and Apartments

A simple concrete and glass structure located on an industrial site between Albert Bridge and Battersea Bridge with a spectacular riverside frontage; an entire working, living and relaxing environment has been created, looking its best when illuminated at night.

From the crumbling back-street approach, one is transported into a crisp, white atmosphere. At the top of a grand flight of stone steps the receptionist sits behind a Nomos table, employees take coffee at the bar seated on Foster barstools, viewing the elegant reception/gallery space and the main office and river beyond.

Huge 'dinosaur' tables stretch out across the vast light-filled studio floor. Each workstation accommodates whole project teams, storage for their drawings and a Totem (a vertical post designed by Foster to house electricity, computer and telephone sockets). Extra meeting tables, Eames' wire chairs and project models are displayed along the glazed river frontage. On the south side a mezzanine floor houses an audio-visual room, slide and technical libraries above with sound-proofed machine workshop and computer rooms below. The main library is fitted to the length and breadth of the back wall, light diffused here by fritted glass.

Upper floors are occupied by glass-fronted luxury apartments with the architect's own home atop the vigorously Foster-designed empire.

ADDRESS 22 Hester Road, London SW11 [7C 76]
CLIENT Petmoor Developments
STRUCTURAL ENGINEER Ove Arup & Partners
SITE AREA 4000 square metres
BUILDING AREA 2000 square metres
BUS 19, 45A, 49, 249, 349 to south side of Battersea Bridge
ACCESS none

Chelsea and Battersea

Foster Associates 1990

Foster Associates 1990

Marco Polo House

This larger-than-life building has been dubbed everything from the liquorice allsort to London's own Legoland. Architectural historians gag at the thought even of entering a discussion about it, but it must be one of the most popular buildings in the city as far as London's inhabitants are concerned. Marco Polo House holds its own as a monument to Post-Modernism with no competition in the immediate vicinity (barring Battersea Power Station). The synthetic cleanliness of the almost injection-moulded form of the exterior is another attraction, as the building looks as if it will never suffer from wear and tear – a quick hose down and it will be as good as new, thanks to a Japanese cladding system called Neo-Paries which has a virtually flawless surface like pure marble. Each panel is barely 2 cm thick. A new glazing system developed by Pilkington meant that each sheet of glass could rest directly on top of another without a frame, all contributing to the sheer surface of the building.

The theme is a simplified classical temple with details blown up out of all proportion. The broken pediments, obviously taken from Philip Johnson's AT&T building in New York, simplify the already simplified, to the extent that there is no indication of how to get inside (Terry Farrell uses this device intentionally at Vauxhall Cross, the new headquarters for MI6) or what occurs inside.

ADDRESS Queenstown Road, SW8 [3F 93]
CLIENT Flaxyard plc
BUS 137, 137A across Chelsea Bridge or 44, 344 from Vauxhall
ACCESS none

Peter Argyrou Associates on behalf of Ian Pollard 1987

Chelsea and Battersea

Peter Argyrou Associates on behalf of Ian Pollard 1987

Vauxhall and Pimlico

Vauxhall Cross

Vauxhall Cross is MI6's new headquarters. Up until now the secret services have been housed inconspicuously in undistinguishable 1960s' office buildings around London. A new image is being developed here.

This is a bespoke (as opposed to a speculative) office building. The brief included the construction of a landscaped river wall and public riverside walkway. Three main blocks, containing nine floors, step back from low-rise bunkers at garden level rising in cold symmetry to a bow window, reminiscent of the river frontage at Charing Cross, but this time crowned with menacing concrete spikes. There is an equal proportion of dark-green glazed curtain walling and precast pigmented concrete panels (each one weighing 5–8 tonnes). It was the largest precast concrete cladding contract to date in the UK. The building is utterly impermeable – the façade allows no insight into the human activities inside. These appearances are by no means deceptive: built into the concrete framework is a 'Faraday Cage' – a mesh which prevents electro-magnetic information from passing in and out of the building. An anonymous site has gained a theatrically ominous building – apt that its neighbour to the west should be the Nine Elms Cold Store.

ADDRESS Albert Embankment, London SE1 [5J 77]
CLIENT Regalian Properties
STRUCTURAL ENGINEER Ove Arup & Partners
CONTRACT VALUE £125 million
SIZE 12,000 square metres (site area)
TUBE Vauxhall – Victoria Line
BR Vauxhall from Waterloo
BUS 2, 2A, 2B, 36, 36B, 77A, 88, 185 to Vauxhall
ACCESS none

Vauxhall and Pimlico

Terry Farrell & Company 1990–1993

Terry Farrell & Company 1990–1993

Clore Gallery, The Tate Gallery

In 1851, 290 oil paintings and 20,000 works on paper by J M W Turner were left to the nation. The collection was fragmented due to flooding in the Tate and to war damage, and as a result much of the work was stored in the Print Room of the British Museum. The daughter of Sir Charles Clore (a dedicated friend and benefactor of the Tate Gallery who sadly died before discussions for a new gallery started) proposed that the works be housed together again, and Stirling and Wilford were appointed as architects in 1979 having recently completed the Staatsgallerie in Stuttgart. It was a triumph, not only as an example of oustanding private patronage to the arts (£1 million was also donated by the Government) but also as a chance for James Stirling, one of Britain's most astounding architects, to create a prominent public building in the capital city.

The brief was to hang 100 of the best paintings permanently, to have reserve galleries, a print room for the works on paper and sketchbooks, a conservation studio and auditorium. The site determined the L-shaped extension, built between Sidney Smith's classical Tate and a red-brick military hospital. The front façade echoes neighbouring materials – red brick set within a honey-coloured stone grid. The intention was to make the Clore 'a garden building … a bit like an orangery', hence its low roof line and attention to landscaping in the foreground. The back of the building is simply yellow brick and obviously designed not to be seen. The façade is strikingly windowless, only two green windows and the entrance penetrate the grid and suggest that something occurs inside.

The entrance hall (in hues of 'Peach' and 'Fragrance') applauds Mannerism in the same way that the National Gallery extension does. The architect uses the staircase to articulate a tight space, making reference to the Scala Regia in the Vatican in Rome. On entering you walk to your left across the hall, then right up the stairs, following the pink

Vauxhall and Pimlico

Stirling Wilford Associates 1980–1985

bannister rail, and then left, back along a landing, orientated once again by the crudely colour-coded arched window next to the entrance to the galleries. According to Chinese mythology, demons only move in straight lines, so zig-zagging pathways are always laid in front gardens.

The galleries themselves are rather conventional in style and proportion but the beige colour of the permanent hanging walls received tremendous criticism when first revealed. The deep red (the same shade that Turner chose to hang his work against) was deemed more appropriate for the reserve galleries. Natural lighting is a success. Many of the paintings inside were painted close to the Thames, and it therefore seemed essential to allow this true light to illuminate them. Light scoops in the ceiling bounce light on to the walls making the middle of the gallery slightly darker than the perimeter. The overall detailing of the building is rather raw but that is cosmetic. When awarded an RIBA National Award in 1988 the jury wrote: 'the rigour with which the rather blandly detailed forms are carried through is commendable'. It is quite evident that the articulation of the spaces has been seriously considered, which is, after all, the architecture.

ADDRESS Millbank, London SW1 [4J 77]
CLIENT Trustees of the Tate Gallery
STRUCTURAL ENGINEER Felix J Samuely & Partners
CONTRACT VALUE £7.7 million (about the cost of one Manet painting)
SIZE 3199 square metres
TUBE Pimlico – Victoria Line
BUS 77A, C10 to Millbank
ACCESS Monday to Saturday, 10.00–17.50, Sunday 14.00–17.50.
Closed on Bank Holidays

Vauxhall and Pimlico

Stirling Wilford Associates 1980–1985

Lambeth Floating Fire Station

Close consultation with the client helped the architect to accommodate an enormous number of facilities into a very tight space. Plant rooms, workshops, locker rooms, a gymnasium and lecture room are housed within the steel hull, and sleeping accommodation, showers, offices and kitchen within a lightweight, steel-framed, aluminium-clad shed structure on top. The floating building is long and low in the water with simple, unostentatious detailing. The complete pontoon was constructed in the Borth Shipyard in Aberystwyth, North Wales, and then towed around the coast and up the River Thames to be moored by Lambeth Bridge.

Vauxhall and Pimlico

ADDRESS off the Albert Embankment, London SE1 [5J 77]
CLIENT Parkman Buck Limited for the London Fire and Civil Defence Authority
CONTRACT VALUE £1.2 million
SIZE 10 by 40 metres
BUS 3, 77, 159, C10 to Lambeth Bridge (Albert Embankment)
ACCESS none

Alsop Lyall & Störmer 1991

Alsop Lyall & Störmer 1991

Lambeth Community Care Centre

The Tomlinson Report of 1992 singles out the Lambeth Community Care Centre. 'We have been impressed by the concept of the "Community Hospital" which has been implemented in West Lambeth, and which provides on a planned basis access to low-intensity care for the patients of a group of general practitioners. We recommend that this model should also be more widely adopted'. It is 'the concept' devised by the Community Health Council which is impressive, i.e. a small-scale partner to the District General Hospital, where patients can be cared for by their own GP in an secluded environment but in the centre of a city. The architect has sensitively positioned bedrooms and a conservatory with a wide terrace running along the length of the upper floor to overlook a garden. The south-facing orientation of these rooms exploits passive solar gain, making them bright and airy. A brick base houses the private consulting rooms on the ground floor and forms a solid street façade, while on the garden side day rooms look out through French windows. The psychology behind the layout of the Care Centre is undoubtedly to be admired. The street façade has an unfortunate nursery school complexion (decorated with floral medallions) which I would sooner see portray the features of this innovative health programme and thus invite curiosity about the benefits of a more imaginative community architecture.

ADDRESS Monkton Street, London SE11 4TX [4A 78]
CLIENT West Lambeth Health Authority
STRUCTURAL ENGINEER Felix J Samuely & Partners
CONTRACT VALUE £955,000 exclusive of furniture and fees
SIZE 1158 square metres
BUS 3, 3B, 159 to Kennington Road
ACCESS limited to patients

Edward Cullinan Architects Limited 1980–1985

Vauxhall and Pimlico

Vauxhall and Pimlico

Edward Cullinan Architects Limited 1980–1985

Richmond House

A seven-storey building conforming in every way to the surrounding architecture, from the heights of the neighbouring buildings to the red brick and stone banding on the rear façade which faces onto Norman Shaw's Old Scotland Yard building. The service stairs are housed within the stumpy yellow brick and grey granite columns on the Whitehall frontage. Heavy stone-mullioned bay windows reflect the austerity of the rest of Whitehall, but are no competition for Lutyens' Cenotaph which sits in the road directly in front. The best aspect is the way that the building sits back from the main road, so that the view down this dramatically wide road (an unusual feature in London) remains unhampered.

Charles Jencks described the scheme as 'Gothick Perpendicular meets Brutalism', which I would say is also a fair assessment of the government in power at the time of its construction.

Vauxhall and Pimlico

ADDRESS 79 Whitehall, London W1 [1J 77]
CLIENT Department of Health and Social Security
CONTRACT VALUE £38.6 million
SIZE 15,000 square metres
TUBE Westminster – District, Circle Lines
BUS 3, 11, 12, 24, 53, 77A, 88, 109, 159, 177X, 184, 196 to Whitehall
ACCESS none

William Whitfield 1988

William Whitfield 1988

Waterloo International Terminal

'The Gateway to Europe' is one of the longest railway stations in the world, with the capacity to handle up to 15 million passengers a year, due to open in July 1994. The architects' ambition was to capture the heritage of heroic engineers such as Isambard Kingdom Brunel, who created large-span, iron-roofed railway stations over a century ago, and to celebrate the Channel Tunnel rail link to the rest of Europe.

Five new tracks were set out by British Rail; these determined the geometry and shape of the whole scheme. The new building is made up of four components. At the bottom, a reinforced-concrete box accommodates the car park which spans the Underground lines and forms the foundation for the Terminal. On top of this concrete box sits a two-storey viaduct supporting the 400-metre-long platforms. This part must bear the weight of the 800-tonne trains and their braking force. Thirdly, brick vaults beneath the existing station are being repaired to accommodate back-up services. The fourth and most prominent component is the roof, although it only comprised 10 per cent of the overall budget. It extends the full length of the 400-metre trains, providing shelter for all the passengers like a vast scaly sleeve. Unfortunately, it does not crash into the existing patchwork of railway sheds but stands an awkward distance from the main Waterloo entrance. However, it happily disregards apartment and office blocks along its length, clipping the corners of any buildings that stand in its way.

The complex structure is essentially a flattened three-pin bowstring arch, distorted to follow the curve and changing width of the platforms. A series of diminishing compressive tubes are employed to cope with any movement. Pressed, profiled, stainless-steel tapered tubes define the bays and give expression to the lightweight structure. In order to avoid cutting 2520 panels of glass to size, at vast expense, a 'loose-fit' glazing system

Nicholas Grimshaw and Partners Limited 1991–1993

Nicholas Grimshaw and Partners Limited 1991–1993

of overlapping standard-size glass sheets had to be devised with a concertina joint to deal with the twist in the structure.

The whole roof system was thoroughly tested before going on site – a 1:1 model was weather tested with the help of high-pressure hoses and an aircraft engine to simulate wind and rain, followed by a 16-week construction dress rehearsal to ensure that everything ran according to plan on site.

Vauxhall and Pimlico

ADDRESS Waterloo Station, London SE1 [2K 77]
CLIENT British Rail
ROOF ENGINEER YRM Anthony Hunt Associates
TRAFFIC AND PASSENGER FLOW Sir Alexander Gibb & Partners
CONTRACT VALUE £120 million
TUBE Waterloo – Northern, Bakerloo Lines
BUS 1, 4, 68, 77, 149, 168, 171, 171A, 176, 188, 501, 502, 505, 507, 511, 513, D1, P11 to Waterloo
ACCESS open; the interior is only open to travellers to Europe

Nicholas Grimshaw and Partners Limited 1991–1993

Vauxhall and Pimlico

Nicholas Grimshaw and Partners Limited 1991–1993

Entertainment Pavilion, Hayward Gallery

A new clause in the gallery's insurance conditions prohibits the consumption of alcohol in places where loaned works of art are on display. This left no space in which to hold functions for sponsors. The problem was solved by building this timber structure (inspired by the traditional barns of the Pennsylvanian Amish sect) which sits like a huge freight container on one of the sculpture balconies overlooking Waterloo Bridge.

Built in 28 days, the entire shed is clad in sterling board and stained a rich burnt red. The interior brims with natural light on a good day when the 4-metre full-height doors on the north elevation are flung open; artificial lighting is by the high-street catalogue store Argos. Interior columns are wrapped in rope to avoid splinters at hand and shoulder level.

The architect has got the most out of the one material by paying attention to finish and detailing, enabling the pavilion to be as self-assured as any so-called permanent structure, particularly the one on which it rests. Sadly, it may only be with us for a few months before a broader strategy for the whole site is implemented in May 1996.

The same architects have refurbished The People's Palace restaurant in the Royal Festival Hall.

ADDRESS South Bank, London SE1 [K1 77]
STRUCTURAL ENGINEER Whitby & Bird
CONTRACT VALUE £52,000
TUBE Waterloo – Bakerloo and Northern Lines (signs to Hayward Gallery)
BUS 1, 4, 26, 68, 76, 77, 149, 168, 171, 171A, 176, 18, 211, 501, 505, 507, 521, D1, P11 to Waterloo
ACCESS open

Vauxhall and Pimlico

Allies and Morrison 1994

Allies and Morrison 1994

West End

Buckingham Palace Ticket Office

Buckingham Palace has started to open its doors to visitors during August and September each year. The brief for a new ticket office called for a demountable, storable structure which could be used for five years. The prefabricated timber office cabin is brought to the site in two parts (mounted on wheels) and bolted together. Birch-faced plywood ribs are bolted to the steel chassis to make the frame and then the whole is clad externally with Western Red Cedar strips and sealed with yacht varnish. It is surrounded by a timber deck which floats on adjustable feet to conceal the wheels of the cabin once it is in position.

A tensile fabric canopy covers the area defined by the edges of the deck. It is supported on two elliptical glulam timber masts (one at either end of the cabin) with a main keel beam running between them. The beam is bolted to the cabin with steel plates which slice into the laminated timber edge above the teller windows. A series of struts attached to the main beam extend outwards horizontally and are tied by vertical tensile cables to concrete blocks in the ground.

This is a building which fits the season and its setting. It uses a vocabulary of details derived from marquees, boats and elegant travelling cases – the cabin alone is like the portmanteau that I imagine Her Majesty might take on holiday.

ADDRESS Lower Grosvenor Place, London SW1 [3F 77]
STRUCTURAL ENGINEER Ove Arup & Partners
TUBE Green Park – Victoria and Piccadilly Lines, then walk across the park to the Canada Gate entrance
BUS 2, 8, 9, 10, 14, 16, 19, 22, 36, 38, 52, 73, 74, 82, 137, 137A to Hyde Park Corner, then walk down Constitution Hill to Buckingham Palace
ACCESS open in August and September only

West End

Michael Hopkins & Partners 1994

Michael Hopkins & Partners 1994

Channel 4 Headquarters

This is a key modern building in the heart of Westminster. Situated in a stagnant corner of Victoria (boldly moving out of the Soho/West End media clique), the Channel 4 building will assist in generating a new spirit in the area. The territory is stalked by the colossal 1960s' Department of the Environment blocks waiting on Death Row, the now rotting corpse of what was Westminster Hospital, the charmless DSS office just down the road and the Royal Horticultural Society buildings (1904 and 1928). Not exactly showbiz potential! However, this new building, comprising a major underground car park, TV studios and offices, a residential development of 100 apartments (by Lyons Sleeman + Hoare) and garden square, should make a considerable impact on its business and residential neighbours by introducing a lively industry to the area which in turn will generate new resources.

In plan, there are four wings around a central garden. The northern and western sides are occcupied by Channel 4 and the southern and eastern sides are residential blocks. The L-shaped offices butt up to the street but a generous recess into the corner has been given over to a dramatic entrance. The approach is across a bridge over what appears to be a glass pool, but is actually the roof to an underground studio. To your left is a stack of boxes (conference rooms) held in an elegant framework of tapered beams; to the right exterior lifts cling to a service tower and transmission antennae (the feather in the cap). The entrance itself is through a concave glass curtain which appears to be hung from a row of curtain claws (as opposed to curtain rings) draped between the two wings and allowing a glimpse of the reception, restaurant and garden beyond.

The exterior walls of the office wings are largely made up of glass and glass blocks, in lower areas clad in a mesh screen to reduce solar gain but

West End

Richard Rogers Partnership 1991–1994

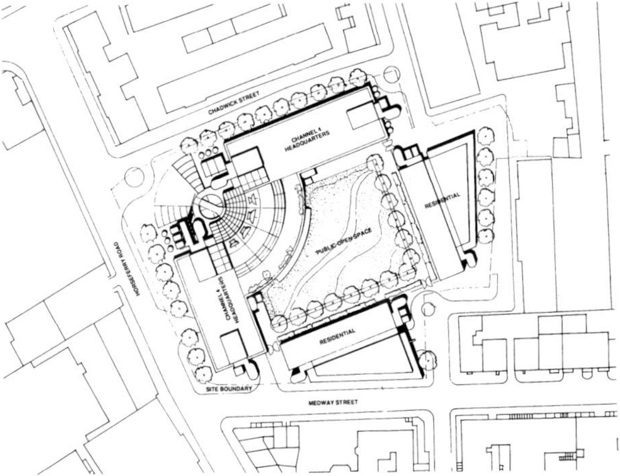
CHADWICK STREET
CHANNEL 4 HEADQUARTERS
RESIDENTIAL
PUBLIC OPEN SPACE
HORSEFERRY ROAD
CHANNEL 4 HEADQUARTERS
RESIDENTIAL
SITE BOUNDARY
MEDWAY STREET

Richard Rogers Partnership 1991–1994

without creating sheer impenetrable surfaces. Elsewhere, cladding is a dull pewter grey aluminium and exposed steel work painted a rich primer red – the exact colour of the Golden Gate Bridge in San Francisco!

The contrast between all the various parts of the building is what makes it so distinctive but the elements work together (from the outside anyway) in that they form a varied, relatively low-level landscape rather than a solid block. The offices are identifiably different from the conference rooms, each part seeming to have a clear agenda, and the entrance holds no bars.

ADDRESS Horseferry Road, London SW1 [4H 77]
STRUCTURAL ENGINEER Ove Arup & Partners
SIZE 15,000 square metres
TUBE St James' Park – District and Circle Lines
BUS 11, 24, 88, 211 to Victoria Street
ACCESS limited

West End

Richard Rogers Partnership 1991–1994

Richard Rogers Partnership 1991–1994

Embankment Place: Charing Cross

The primary development of this strategic piece of city planning is 32,000 square metres of office space using the air rights above Charing Cross Station. It is one of the most prominent sites in London. Seven to nine storeys are suspended above the tracks, insulating the offices from the clattering railway. While nine pairs of columns grew out of the platforms to support lofty bowstring arches, working hours were restricted to between one and four in the morning so that the 120,000 people that pass through the station daily could continue to do so undisturbed.

The masterplan extends to 'traffic management' (Cardboard City clearance) in Embankment Place, the extension of the Hungerford Bridge onto the concourse of Charing Cross Station (an intimidating blind passageway which then thankfully opens out with views on to Villiers Street), the relocation of the Players' Theatre, adjustments to Embankment Gardens and to the station forecourt, and the revitalisation of Villiers Street into a busy pedestrianised shopping and eating thoroughfare. Craven Passage, beneath the station, has also been hosed down and transformed into a shopping arcade – still largely vacant.

Design details are consistent, from ornament right through to finishes, continuing with the pretence that brick cladding reflects the street scale and granite cladding reflects the scale of the other riverside buildings. Cartoon-like classical references can be found in many of the decorative motifs such as the bulging Doric columns on the platforms and the pale green metalwork mimicking copper roofs. The giant glazed railway-shed arches crouch between service towers positioned at the four corners. At the top of each tower is a stunning and unique view across London – unfortunately reserved exclusively for the occupants of executive suites.

New exits are currently being made at the river end of the platforms so that there is direct access from Embankment Station and Whitehall.

West End

Terry Farrell & Company 1987–1990

For many critics, the monumental scheme respects the existing infrastructure. It certainly dominates the skyline along a prominent part of the river and Farrell seems adamant that an anticipated 6500 new occupants, given time, will undoubtedly transform the area. Transform or homogenise?

ADDRESS Villiers Street, London WC2 [1J 77]
CLIENT Greycoat Developers
STRUCTURAL ENGINEER Ove Arup & Partners
CONTRACT VALUE £100 million
SIZE 32,000 square metres (masterplan area)
TUBE Embankment – District, Circle Lines; Charing Cross – Northern, Bakerloo, Jubilee Lines
BUS 1, 4, 6, 9, 11, 13, 15, 15B, X15, 77A, 176, 177, 501, 502, 505, 513 to the Strand
ACCESS open

West End

Terry Farrell & Company 1987–1990

West End

Terry Farrell & Company 1987–1990

The Sainsbury Wing, National Gallery

A brief history of the site: acquired by HM Government in 1959 to provide an extension for the National Gallery, lack of funds always prevented any development until 1980 when the then Secretary of State, Michael Heseltine, proposed a public competition to develop the site commercially with galleries on the upper floors. Ahrends, Burton & Koralek were chosen to produce designs. Their proposals were received like a fishbone stuck in the throat but planning permission was sought. The Prince of Wales finally knocked ABK's scheme on the head in 1984 when he denounced it as 'a monstrous carbuncle on the face of a much-loved and elegant friend' (the architect's quotable quote of the 1980s). Not surprisingly, planning permission was refused and the Government was let off the hook.

The present scheme was conceived early in 1985. Private donors, namely the Sainsbury brothers, came to the rescue and offered to fund a new extension. In January 1986 Venturi, Scott Brown's designs were selected and everyone breathed a sigh of relief when the Prince sealed his approval by laying the foundation stone exactly two years later.

The new wing houses the collection of early Italian Renaissance and Northern European paintings and temporary exhibitions in 16 daylit galleries, a lecture theatre, gallery shop and restaurant, meeting rooms and an interactive information centre. The main construction is a steel and concrete frame clad in the same Portland stone as the original building (designed by William Wilkins in 1838).

The aesthetics of the building derive from Venturi's Post-Modern theories of reinterpreting the past and placing it in the present. All of Wilkins' classical elements have been reproduced on the new façade and then dissected. Inside, the grand stairway in charcoal black granite has a stately presence and the vast arched steel trusses above, mimicking the parts of

West End

Venturi, Scott Brown & Associates, Inc. 1988–1991

a coarse Victorian train shed, are just some of many incongruities which lurk suspiciously in the building. The main gallery spaces symbolise the kinds of 15th-century Tuscan palace rooms in which many of the paintings would originally have been housed. Unfortunately the cool grey walls, American white oak floors and skirting, arch surrounds and large decorative columns in *pietra serena* (Italian sandstone) are not reminiscent of the Dutch domestic interiors where many of the other works would have been found. Surely the purpose of the building was to display these exceptional works of art within a modern context, not to play timidly with symbols from other architectures.

Venturi's own words sum up the building and his attitude towards his architecture: 'it is very sophisticated. You have to be "cultured" to like it.' How many of those whom he refers to as 'the relatively unsophisticated people' who visit the gallery will swallow that?

ADDRESS The National Gallery, Trafalgar Square, London SW1 [1H 77]
CLIENT National Gallery Services
ASSOCIATED UK ARCHITECT Sheppard Robson Architects
STRUCTURAL ENGINEER Ove Arup & Partners
DONORS Lord Sainsbury of Preston Candover, the Hon. Simon Sainsbury, the Hon. Timothy Sainsbury, MP
CONTRACT VALUE £35.5 million
SIZE 11,150 square metres gross
TUBE Charing Cross – Northern, Bakerloo, Jubilee Lines
BUS 3, 6, 9, 11, 12, 13, 15, 15B, X15, 24, 29, 30, 53, 53X, 77A, 88, 94, 109, 139, 159, 176, 177, 184, 196 to Trafalgar Square
ACCESS Monday to Saturday, 10.00–18.00; Sunday, 14.00–18.00. Closed on Bank Holidays

West End

Venturi, Scott Brown & Associates, Inc. 1988–1991

West End

Venturi, Scott Brown & Associates, Inc. 1988–1991

The Sackler Galleries, Royal Academy

Sir Norman Foster adds his name to a short but distinguished list of architects who have contributed to the evolution of the Royal Academy. Burlington House was built in 1666. The front elevation was remodelled by Colen Campbell from 1717–1720, with a garden façade by Samuel Ware added in 1815 and a gallery extension in 1867 by Sidney Smirke. A gap, almost 5 metres wide, between the garden façade and Smirke's extension is the site for Foster's contribution which provides new circulation up to the previously isolated Diploma Galleries on the third storey.

From the atmosphere of a narrow Victorian alley-way at ground level, visitors are rapidly transported by a glass-walled, hydraulic lift up to a new public space. The journey up through three floors past the newly renovated exteriors by Smirke and Ware is breathtaking (it could quite easily be 30 floors). At the top you are dazzled by bright white light through translucent glass all around, and the vast, sculpted head of a Greek god resting on the parapet of Smirke's façade creates a bizarre and dramatic sense of scale and great distance.

Stepping out of the lift into the public gallery and meeting place, you are free to wander and look at Gibson's sculptures which sit along the same parapet. At the end, across a delicate glass bridge, is a cool, open ante-room where you can sit and view the Royal Academy's most valuable possession, Michelangelo's 'Virgin and Child with Infant St. John', and catch another look back along the sculpture gallery. This series of spaces is simply defined by light and subtle changes in materials, which float structurally independent between the old buildings. Glazed edges around the floor surfaces help to make this distinction between the old and new building techniques.

The three Diploma Galleries (now the Sackler Galleries) were gutted, flat roofs demolished and two barrel-vaulted ceilings installed with roof

Foster Associates 1989–1991

West End

Foster Associates 1989–1991

lights. As a conservation measure, air quality is carefully controlled; air is distributed very slowly across the art works and wall surfaces. Roof lights provide UV filtration and natural light is controlled by fritted glass and a series of louvres which open and close depending on the intensity of light. This solution has proved unsatisfactory and is currently being reassessed.

Visitors can leave the galleries by descending the staircase. It has the elegant sweep of a grand stairway but, like a fire escape, it provides a winding route down through the gap with views through the windows of the old garden façade into the offices of the gallery. There is an underground atmosphere when you look up and see shadows of footsteps through the sand-blasted glass stair treads over your head.

Extensive use of different types of glass (a Foster trademark) has allowed as much natural light as possible to filter down through the gap while the vertical movement through it allows us to see the old façades in a new and more detailed way, giving a whole new meaning to scale and proportion, comfort without upholstery, conservation without conservatism.

ADDRESS The Royal Academy of Arts, Piccadilly, London W1 [1F 77]
CLIENT The Royal Academy of Arts
STRUCTURAL ENGINEER YRM Anthony Hunt Associates
HISTORIC BUILDINGS CONSULTANT Julian Harrap Associates
CONTRACT VALUE £5.2 million
TUBE Piccadilly Circus – Piccadilly, Bakerloo Lines; Green Park – Piccadilly, Victoria Lines
BUS 19, 38, 55
ACCESS 10.00–17.30, every day

West End

Foster Associates 1989–1991

West End

Foster Associates 1989–1991

Osho Gallery, The Economist Building

In the heart of St James's, an area associated with shopping and dining out rather than a tranquil spot for contemplation, a new gallery has been embedded in the the ground floor of Alison and Peter Smithson's listed Economist Building. Osho International, a publishing house dedicated to spreading the word of the mystic Osho, wanted a gallery space 'to give expression to the silence, grace and spaciousness of meditation'. The architects responded by creating a series of flexible, light, open spaces where exhibitions can be held, books and artefacts can be displayed, and quiet converstations can be had against the background murmur of a falling water feature.

All the interior surfaces are made from light materials: walls are white-painted plaster; the rear gallery has a white Portuguese limestone floor; Canadian maple timber is used on the floor of the front gallery and for all the joinery and furniture.

Changing floor and ceiling levels and a tight floor plan have created an ætherial crypt-like space which faces directly on to the street from within one of London's most admired modern buildings. This has been achieved by a thorough use of good materials and the maintenance of natural light while outside noise is deadened by adding secondary glazing to the elevations.

ADDRESS St James's Street, London W1 [1G 77]
CLIENT Osho International
STRUCTURAL ENGINEER YRM Anthony Hunt Associates
TUBE Piccadilly – Piccadilly Line
BUS 9, 14, 19, 22, 38 to Piccadilly (get off near the Royal Academy)
ACCESS open Monday to Saturday 10.00–18.00

West End

Stanton Williams 1994

Stanton Williams 1994

Imagination Building

No strip-lighting, no suspended ceilings, no air-conditioning: this is no ordinary office building. Architects, writers, film and video producers, designers, theatre and lighting technicians, engineers, photographers, composers and production managers, all from one organization, Imagination, reside under one roof, and it is no ordinary roof. This outstanding refurbishment of a less-than-outstanding Edwardian school represents the innovative nature of Imagination in the field of design and promotion.

The original building consisted of a five-storey crescent block on Store Street and a parallel block behind, divided by a cluttered central courtyard. Herron Associates gutted the buildings, created a basement level to house sound and photographic studios and a gymnasium, then covered the cleared courtyard and adjacent buildings with a dramatic polymer-coated membrane, adding another 2000 square metres of floor space. Tent-like structures have been a preoccupation of Ron Herron's since the 1960s and the days of Archigram. At last a little bit of this fantasy has become reality.

On arrival one is met by an unassuming Edwardian façade and a modest reception/exhibition area. But past the desk through the porthole of pale oak doors a luminosity seeps out. Beyond these doors is the courtyard where the eye is drawn up through 126 metres of bright, natural light, punctuated at diagonals by aluminium bridges that link the two blocks. Beyond this floats the translucent roof.

The fabric membrane proved to be one-third the cost and one-sixth of the weight of glazing with a considerably finer quality of light, enhanced by tungsten halogen lighting elsewhere in the building. The roof panels were made in two long sections, clamped around the edges onto a steel grid, and at points in mid-span aluminium tree-like structures stress the fabric so that it is taut. There is an additional liner membrane to reduce

West End

Herron Associates 1989

Herron Associates 1989

any risk of condensation. You can get a good detailed view of this technical feat from what used to be the roof-top playground and is now a public gallery space, sheltered by the canopy and glazed walls.

The original structures have barely been tampered with; the brickwork is painted brilliant white, new services and wall-to-wall stainless-steel bathroom facilities installed. Office floors have generally been left open with views across the atrium through existing window openings. A thoroughly modern and industrious atmosphere has grown out of the substance of the old building by the magnificent and serene articulation of innovative technology.

Appropriately, the outside of the roof structure can be seen, like a huge snow drift, from the terrace of the Architectural Association in Bedford Square.

ADDRESS Store Street, London WC1 [5H 61]
CLIENT Imagination (Design and Communication)
STRUCTURAL ENGINEER Buro Happold Consulting Engineers
CONTRACT VALUE £4.5 million
SIZE 20,000 square metres
TUBE Tottenham Court Road – Central, Northern Lines; Goodge Street – Northern Line
BUS 10, 14, 24, 29, 73, 134 to Tottenham Court Road
ACCESS only when there is an exhibition on. Telephone first on 0171–323 3300

West End

Herron Associates 1989

Herron Associates 1989

Camden and Islington

J Sainsbury's Supermarket

The site, where the ABC Bakery once stood, is bounded by the Regent's Canal, Camden Street, Camden Road and Kentish Town Road. It is a mixed development covering an entire block and comprises the supermarket, a crèche, small workshops, ten housing units, a bedsit flat and a one-bedroom maisonette.

The scale of the existing busy streets determined the size and proportions of the main Camden Road frontage – the bays set out to mirror the widths of the listed Georgian houses opposite. The supermarket is based on the 'market hall' structure – a column-free retail floor and a high curved ceiling with a clear span of 43.2 metres. This is achieved by a central span supported by cantilevers which are in turn counter balanced by tie-down rods. The open space allows for changes in retail methods, but at present it contains a devastatingly standard shop interior.

The structural form is revealed in the end elevations. Each element is designed to be functional so there was close co-operation between the architect and the engineer – often swapping roles, the architect calculating loads and inventing working parts and the engineer attempting to devise forms for the element. As a result, both tend to over-compensate for their efforts. Each joint is expressed as a separate part to help describe the process of construction.

It was possible for all structural elements to be visible because of a new form of fire protection – an epoxy/ceramic material, previously used on North Sea oil rigs but never before on a major building. It revolutionizes the use of exposed steelwork and enhances Grimshaw's preoccupation as architect/engineer. All façades are detailed in aluminium, steel and glass.

The cocoon-like residential units sit, aluminium clad, along a 10-metre wide strip parallel to the canal like loading bays for a ship. In order to

Nicholas Grimshaw and Partners Limited 1988

Nicholas Grimshaw and Partners Limited 1988

exclude noise from the supermarket car park behind, a tall open-plan was devised, windowless at the back but top-lit and fronted by a north-facing double-height glazed wall incorporating a vertical sliding industrial door, which when opened allows the outdoors into the dining area of the house. The houses are built from concrete blockwork with felt covered timber roofs and an external cladding of aluminium 'rainscreen' panels.

ADDRESS Camden Road, London NW1 [6H 45]
CLIENT J Sainsbury's plc
STRUCTURAL ENGINEER Kenchington Little and Partners
CONTRACT VALUE £15 million
SIZE OF SUPERMARKET 1300 square metres
TUBE Camden Town – Northern Line
BUS 24, 27, 29, 31, 68, 134, 135, 168, 214, 253, 274, C2 to Camden High Street
ACCESS open

Nicholas Grimshaw and Partners Limited 1988

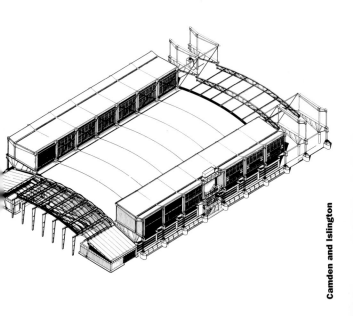

Camden and Islington

Nicholas Grimshaw and Partners Limited 1988

JS Pathology Laboratory

This project was executed when Max Hutchinson was also making preparations to take office as president of the RIBA (1989). It was a more than feverish time. JS Pathology, the largest private pathology laboratory in Europe, wanted to bring its 300 employees together under one roof. The new building houses all testing facilities.

The front elevation rests on a row of four thin columns which pierce the blue glazed first and second floor levels protruding at the top to support a concrete and glass canopy. The ground floor has a recessed brick wall defining the entrance (a façade reminiscent of office buildings of the 1930s and 1950s). The brick sides and canal frontage are surpisingly successful. acheiving the warmth of the 19th-century warehouse across the canal without the crudity of so much modern brick render.

The central dazzling feature, a lightweight staircase, cuts a light-filled gorge from the front through to the rear (canal side) of the building, reaching forth like Jacob's Ladder. A gradual taper in plan distorts the perspective, intensifying the drama of the steps which seem to reach the sky. To the left is a sheer, sloping, glacial screen wall allowing views and natural light into the labs. The solid right-hand side of the stairway accommodates services. Internally, the architect has developed 1980s' devices to create an uplifting working environment.

ADDRESS Jamestown Road, London NW1 [1F 61]
STRUCTURAL ENGINEER Alan Baxter Associates
CONTRACT VALUE £15 million
TUBE Camden Town – Northern Line
BUS 24, 27, 29, 31, 68, 134, 168, 214, 253, 274, C2 to Camden High Street
ACCESS none

Hutchinson & Partners 1991

Camden and Islington

Hutchinson & Partners 1991

TV-AM Building

Now occupied by MTV, after TV-AM lost its broadcasting franchise at the end of 1992, this building is still considered to be a high point of British Post-modernism – it was a reaction against the traditional appearance of so many office buildings and an attempt to cheer up a country at an economic low. The result is a stage set made from washing-up liquid bottles and sticky-backed plastic in the *Blue Peter* style of building.

The TV studios are sandwiched in three layers from the front façade on Hawley Crescent with an atrium in the middle and the Regent's Canal at the back. The front is a curving, windowless wall of corrugated steel cladding which runs in ever-decreasing bands towards the top (some tenuous reference to a classical hierarchy), terminated at each end by the TV-AM logo (now covered by blue discs). The entrance is defined by an arch of massive proportions and made from a knot of aluminium tubes drawn from the façade and tied with a neon keystone. More of the same continues inside.

The canal façade can be seen from Camden Lock and displays the famous egg-cup finials on the saw-toothed factory roof line. The eggs were made from glass fibre in the architect's own office.

The building has managed to capture people's attention for as long as the television station.

ADDRESS Hawley Crescent, London NW1 [7F 45]
CLIENT TV-AM Television Studios
CONTRACT VALUE £40 per square foot
TUBE Camden Town – Northern Line
BUS 24, 27, 29, 31, 68, 134, 135, 168, 214, 253, 274, C2 to Camden High Street
ACCESS none

Terry Farrell & Company 1983

Camden and Islington

Terry Farrell & Company 1983

David Wild's House

No. 44, Wild's own house, completed first (built by himself with help from some of his students at South Bank Polytechnic), was proposed as a prototype housing unit. Wild's idea of the home is based on a cave, which has private territory with cosy spaces at the back while its mouth gapes wide to let in light but is partially sheltered by trees. The architect says that he would not want to live in a glass box because he likes to feel safe and enclosed but at the same time wishes to have a view of the world around him. These primitive attributes are reinforced by more recent architectural history and the influence of Adolf Loos on Wild's work. Loos said: 'the building should be dumb on the outside and reveal its wealth only on the inside'. This is certainly true of No. 44 where the large front window is set back from a flat, rendered façade creating a discreet transition between house and street. Once inside you enter a rich but uncluttered world of objects, paintings and colours, each with a personal story.

A reinforced-concrete frame cast *in situ* with precast-concrete floor planks and block infill forms the load-bearing shell structure which occupies two thirds of the site. The gap down the right-hand side of the house allows light to reach inside from another angle (the stairs are located this side) and into the back garden. The plan is a double square, 5.4 x 10.8 metres, with a 3.6 metre square central space marked out by concrete columns which contains the hearth, the heart of the house. Behind the hearth a dog-leg stair, lined with bookcases, links all the floors. The ground floor accommodates children's bedrooms and the entrance; above this is the one-and-a-half-storey main living space at the front, with oak floors and white walls, and an open kitchen at the back. On a third storey is the master bedroom and bathroom at the back, and a fourth studio floor leads onto an outdoor roof terrace.

There is an intrinsic relationship between the inside and the outside.

David Wild 1989, 1984

David Wild 1989, 1984

The whole project is sited around a poplar tree in the front, acting as a foil for the corner concrete column of the façade and softening the hard lines of the interior space. Unfortunately, the original tree died after completion of the house, but another has been grown in its place. Another tragedy hit the house in 1987 when a mechanism in the hearth flue caused its chimney to catch fire, resulting in considerable damage to the stair core and to a lifetime's slide collection. It has been restored to its former state with only traces of black soot on book jackets to tell the tale. Thereafter, in the Japanese tradition, a small pond with running water was installed by the entrance to keep evil spirits at bay.

No. 42, next door, was built to a brief for a specific client. The internal spaces are less intricate than those of No. 44, with a double-height space on the first floor, a steel-framed mezzanine bedroom level at the back and a hearth at the centre following many of the same rules as No. 44. A row of columns runs through the middle of the plan, a central column supporting a low pitched roof. There are no outdoor terraces but the garden at the back is more accessible.

Both houses demonstrate an intelligent response to the past without copying its forms.

ADDRESS 42 and 44 Rochester Place, London NW1 [6G 45]
CLIENT David Wild
CONTRACT VALUE No. 42 – £160,000 (1989), No. 44 – £35,000 (1984)
SIZE No. 42 – 158 square metres, No. 44 – 150 square metres
BUILT No. 42 – 1989, No. 44 – 1984
TUBE Camden Town – Northern Line
BUS 29, 253 to Camden Road
ACCESS none

David Wild 1989, 1984

David Wild 1989, 1984

One Off Studio and Showroom

Ron Arad Associates (architecture and design offices) and One Off Limited (furniture workshops) moved into these courtyard premises while it was still a collection of derelict sheds and then designed and built the present showroom and offices around themselves.

Entering the showroom from the rusty fire-escape stairway is like walking inside the belly of a whale and finding it full of swallowed treasure. To view Arad's gleaming steel furniture, you wander around the creaking landscaped timber floor which scoops upwards at the back to make a hill, creating a division between the showroom and the office beyond. Space under the hill houses the air-handling unit for the air-conditioning bridge which links the showroom to a small mezzanine at the back of the long shed. The office space is covered in a tensioned fabric and expanded metal shell structure (Expamet). The columns along the right-hand side not only support the roof but their calligraphic shapes (from the One Off alphabet) act as a radial track for the industrial PVC windows. The edges are stiffened with a sprung steel frame so that they can be fixed in any position along the curve of the column.

You can check out Arad's furniture and interior design in action at the two Belgo restaurants. The first is a few doors down on Chalk Farm Road while the latest sensation in providing fantastic cheap Belgian food for the masses is Belgo Central, in Covent Garden on the corner of Earlham and Shelton Streets.

ADDRESS 62 Chalk Farm Road, London NW1 [7E 44]
STRUCTURAL ENGINEER Neil Thomas at Atelier One
TUBE Chalk Farm – Northern Line
BUS 31, 68, 168 to Chalk Farm Road
ACCESS to showroom

Ron Arad and Alison Brooks 1991

Camden and Islington

Ron Arad and Alison Brooks 1991

Surgery

You could easily mistake this building for a Swiss alpine chalet but in fact it is a new general practice surgery, on the site of the old surgery and adjoining car park. In order to maintain the precious parking space, the building evolved from the use of Vierendeel beams which spanned the car-park deck in one gesture, squatting on low, stumpy concrete columns.

The structure had to be low-cost and low-maintenance, hence the use of largely prefabricated building parts: a steel main frame with precast-concrete plank floors, unpainted timber weather-boarding on exterior walls, and a roof made of a sandwich of galvanised aluminium and layers of insulation. The curved roof seems to slide out to the sides like wings unfolding, but is held in place on each side by v-shaped brackets. Inside, the effect of the sliding roof has created a barrel-vault, the highest point (containing skylights) covering the waiting room at the centre of the plan. Tensile sails make the walls of the waiting area, separating it from the corridor to the offices and consulting rooms which run around the perimeter of the building. The surgery is unmistakeable from the outside, especially because of the distinctive perforated steel ramp and the way that the building provides a contrasting footing for the tower block.

ADDRESS 111 Adelaide Road, London NW3 [7B 44]
CLIENT Drs M D Peters, Frances A Loughridge, W J Clayton, I K Sienkowski
STRUCTURAL ENGINEER David Powell Edmondson & Partners
CONTRACT VALUE £610,421
SIZE 476 square metres
TUBE Chalk Farm – Northern Line
BUS 31 to Adelaide Road
ACCESS surgery hours

Camden and Islington

Pentarch 1992

Customs and Public Health Building

Part of an £8 million reconstruction of Willesden freight depot, this building is for the inspection of freight which will be travelling through the Channel Tunnel. It is situated next to the west coast mainline, approximately 5 miles north out of Euston Station – stopping at all stations to Glasgow (Watford, Birmingham, Crewe, Manchester, etc.). It is only possible to view the building from a train as security at the depot is tight, so you get an Intercity glance, unless there are leaves on the line.

'Viewing at high speed' has informed the structure so that it is instantly recognizable. In this case form does not follow function as the architects claim. The official inspection of freight is surely not for public consumption. The site follows the function and the form creates a distraction. The building clearly has a front and a back but it is not clear which is which. A curved, corrugated-steel wall, with glazed slots cut out to reveal internal stairways (allowing natural light into the top-floor offices), is displayed as the front to passing passenger trains. Freight is handled at ground level at the back. However, the profile of the structure suggests that front and back should be perceived the opposite way around. This duality arising from the extruded form occurs at Tottenham Hale Station (in a similar genre and a source of inspiration for this building). Could this be the shape of the railway siding buildings of the future?

ADDRESS Willesden Freight Depot, Willesden Junction [3B 58]
CLIENT British Rail Freight Distribution
CONTRACT VALUE £1.4 million
SIZE 1450 square metres
TRAIN any train directed north/west coast
ACCESS none

Camden and Islington

Architecture and Design Group, British Rail 1993

Architecture and Design Group, British Rail 1993

31 Corsica Street

A vast warehouse footprint and its simple structure provide the shell for a mixture of spectacular living and working spaces. The building has been split, the dividing wall forming a service core. The front half now accommodates four apartments with studio/office space on the whole of the ground floor.

The domestic interior is a beautifully executed exercise in modern family living. The spaces are essentially simple, but the configuration of the apartment as a whole is difficult to describe because of the ingenious devices that have been created to maximise natural light while maintaining a warm atmosphere in the large, white spaces.

You enter an open general living area, lined with the warehouse windows along one side and windows facing on to an indoor swimming pool on the other. The pool bounces light from roof terrace windows above through to the living space. There is none of the self-conscious detailing which plagues so many modern interiors, simply elegant inventiveness. The catalogue of original details (generally custom-made using materials such as marble, glass, wood and steel) and the ideas generated by the concept of a family-oriented living and working space are endless.

Bedrooms are tucked away discretely underneath the main space like a ship's cabins; beds are raised on mezzanines to make use of the floor-to-ceiling height while allowing natural light into the back of the rooms.

ADDRESS 31 Corsica Street, London N5 [6B 46]
CLIENT Richard Paxton and Heidi Locher
TUBE Highbury and Islington – Victoria Line
BUS 4, 19, 30, 43, 279 to Highbury Fields
ACCESS none

Paxton Locher Architects 1991

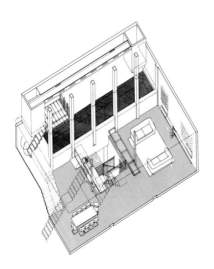

Camden and Islington

Paxton Locher Architects 1991

Private House

This building represents one architect's concept of how a family home might operate and be occupied in the 1990s. It is a four-storey house built from scratch for approximately the same cost as buying a property of a similar size in the area. The result is not a gutted interior with maintained old street façade affair, but a an open plan covering four storeys and wrapped in a glass hood with rigorous attention to detail throughout, from the size of the letterbox to the type of glazing system employed. Each component illustrates changing patterns of living, with the flexibility to adapt to future requirements within the confines of a slow-moving, traditional street pattern.

The south-facing lot is protected front and back by mature trees and flanked by buildings of different scales and characters. Islington Borough Planning Department supported the design concept on the conditions that it did not impinge in any way on the neighbouring house, that the trees were retained and that the entire job was supervised by Future Systems alone to ensure that enduring qualities of detailing and finish (particularly of the exterior) were not jeopardised.

The main construction is steel-framed with in-situ concrete floor decks. The front elevation is made of glass blocks (to maintain a degree of privacy) concealing a triple-height entrance hall. The rear of the house is a 50° slope of double-glazed Planar glass (with openable windows) allowing an unobstructed view from all floors into a sculpted garden. Shading from intense solar-heat gain on this side of the house is provided by the trees and white blinds fixed to the internal face of the glass. In the winter the house is passively heated by solar gain with additional heating provided by conventional radiators.

Any core services that require a modicum of privacy or simply need to be hidden away, such as bathrooms and storage, are housed in free-

Future Systems 1994

standing coloured units which float in unpartitioned floor spaces.

The range of materials and components used has been kept to a minimum – glass envelope, extruded aluminium sections as bracing, ceramic floor tiles. The absence of any skirting boards or architraves has resulted in precise treatment of how two finishes meet, often separated by a third in order to define the role and emphasise the quality of each finish.

This house is a landmark domestic building. Not only is it the first permanent structure to be built in London by this firm of architects but it challenged conventional planning regulations and a sensitive conservation area ... succesfully.

ADDRESS 40 Douglas Road, London N1 [7C 46]
CLIENTS Debra Hauer and Jeremy King
STRUCTURAL ENGINEER Anthony Hunt Associates
SIZE 215 square metres
TUBE Highbury and Islington – Victoria Line
BUS 38, 56, 73, 171A, 271 to Essex Road
ACCESS absolutely none; this is a private family home

Future Systems 1994

Lisson Grove and Hampstead

The Lisson Gallery

The new Lisson Gallery is like a section of the street stripped bare. Each of its four storeys strictly corresponds in height to neighbouring buildings. The façades on the ground- and first-floor galleries have been peeled away to reveal the guts of the building through floor-to-ceiling-height square glass panels which can slide back to enable large works to be moved in and out of the gallery. The second and third storeys are occupied by flats with sheer concrete façades to allow some privacy from the school playground across the street.

Each of the basement, ground and first floors provides a 7-metre squared space linked by an atelier-type stairway to the side. This arrangement allows smaller shows to be exhibited in a single space or for full retrospectives to flow around the entire building. The route begins in the side entrance of the old Lisson Gallery on Lisson Street which is linked to the new space by a long reception corridor. The journey becomes a succession of discoveries, exiting onto the adjacent Bell Street. This 'possession of the space by the visitor', as Fretton calls it, makes the gallery an integral part of a varied community, helping to break down the prejudices on which many art galleries thrive.

ADDRESS 52 Bell Street, London NW1 [5C 60]
CLIENT Lisson Gallery London Limited
STRUCTURAL ENGINEER Price & Myers
CONTRACT VALUE £500,000 approximately
TUBE Edgware Road – District, Circle, Hammersmith and City Lines
BUS 6, 7, 8, 15, 16, 16A, 18, 27, 36 to Edgware Road
ACCESS Monday–Friday, 10.00–18.00; Saturday 10.00–13.00

Lisson Grove and Hampstead

Tony Fretton Architects 1990

Tony Fretton Architects 1990

The Mound Stand, Lord's Cricket Ground

At the end of the 1980s, several architectural journals nominated this project as the 'best' building of the decade. Perhaps this is because it dealt with so many different types of building techniques: the restoration and completion of the existing brick arcade built by Thomas and Frank Verity in 1898 at ground level, the cantilevered steel-framed decks above, and the tent structure on the roof. These involve three diverse technologies and all are executed with the utmost precision. Each layer of the stand is clearly visible from St. John's Wood Road, so that the construction can be logically understood. There are no disguises.

The Marylebone Cricket Club, in its stubbornly traditional way, still distinguishes between types of spectators which in turn informed Hopkins' design. The general public sit in the terraces on the lowest level, box proprietors on a cantilevered promenade (all in corporate ownership except one private box belonging to Paul Getty, Junior, who funded half of the project), and members and debenture holders have access to an open upper promenade beneath the fabric roof – 4500 spectators in all. The atmosphere on the top deck harks back to the quintessentially British scene of a marquee pitched on the village green with spectators scoffing cucumber sandwiches and sipping cups of tea.

The structure that supports the PVC-coated fabric roof is also strongly reminiscent of the rigging on a boat – it is supported by six vertical masts and a series of projecting steel booms with steel cables that tie down into concrete piles at the back of the stand and onto the front of the cantilevered promenade to achieve overall stability.

The superstructure, i.e. that of the cantilevered promenade and boxes, was determined by the thin columns which could not be allowed to obscure the view onto the pitch from the terraces underneath. A spine

Michael Hopkins & Partners 1985–1987

Lisson Grove and Hampstead

Michael Hopkins & Partners 1985–1987

girder runs along the centre of the plan supported by hollow columns (masts for the roof slot inside) set every 18.3 metres along the terrace. Tapered girders cantilever either side of the spine, like ribs, to hold a metal deck and a 160 mm concrete slab for seating and enclosures at the rear. The boxes have an appropriately old school changing room feel to them with fair-faced blockwork walls and simple glazed doors which fold back to frame the pitch. On the same level but overlooking St. John's Wood Road there are private dining rooms and lavatories enclosed by glass bricks to admit light while obscuring the activities from passers-by.

One of the pleasures of the building is that there was no need to insulate or make the decks watertight as it is only fully occupied on eight, fair-weather days of the year. If it should rain, terrace spectators can shelter under the huge Verity arches and have a drink at one of the bars while members and their guests promenade the top deck.

Lisson Grove and Hampstead

ADDRESS St John's Wood Road, London NW8 [4B 60]
CLIENT Marylebone Cricket Club
STRUCTURAL ENGINEER Ove Arup & Partners
BUILT Phase 1 – 1985–1986; Phase 2 – 1986–1987
TUBE St. John's Wood – Jubilee Line
BUS 13, 82, 113, 274 to Lord's
ACCESS seasonal

Michael Hopkins & Partners 1985–1987

Lisson Grove and Hampstead

Michael Hopkins & Partners 1985–1987

Mill Lane Gardening Project

In 1962 Walter Segal was confronted with the problem of providing temporary accommodation for his family while their house was being rebuilt. At a materials cost of £800 (£6500 today) and completed in two weeks, the first Segal self-build 80-square-metre house still stands in the garden of the Highgate house. The key to the success of the building was the rigorous simplification of the construction process: one person with basic carpentry skills could carry out the work (with perhaps the exception of services and roofing). Segal's system is based on a modular grid determined by the sizes of standard materials – ideally these could be disassembled and resold. The frame is timber, clad in woodwool, faced with roofing felt on the exterior and chipboard waste paper inside. The roof is flat (avoiding the use of scaffolding) surfaced with felt and held down by bricks and 35 mm of water. Thirty years later, the building would still pass tests for water penetration or structural failure. Details such as using stainless rather than mild steel bolts and timber jointing rather than nail plate joints (too much movement) have been adopted by many subsequent schemes.

Five per cent of new housing stock in Great Britain is accounted for by self-build – the figure would be far greater if the political establishment could learn to appreciate the method's merits. Homes can be built for about one third of usual cost. The Walter Segal Self-Build Trust was set up in 1988 to continue Segal's work after his death in 1985. The Trust's aim is to help people with limited means to build themselves homes or work on community projects, such as at Mill Lane. What was intended as temporary accommodation has developed into forms of permanent housing where families can build their own environments from start to finish, led by their own programme and with the ability to extend and change it as they wish.

Lisson Grove and Hampstead

Simon Yauner Architects 1992

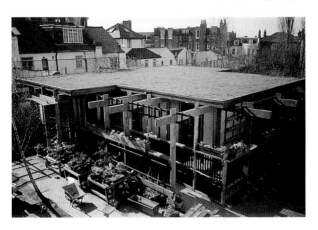

Simon Yauner Architects 1992

The Mill Lane Gardening Project is a centre for adults with learning difficulties. The land is owned by Camden Council but had been deserted for years. A corner of the site was allocated to CSMH for a gardening project. By the end of 1992 the 'trainees' and a number of volunteers had aquired more than just green fingers. The building of the centre was carried out by the users themselves so that the construction process became an integral part of their training. Simon Yauner and his engineer, Rene Weisner, developed the design: discontinuous construction allowing movement between layers. Stephen Backes, a carpenter and welder, was employed to supervise the site and train the volunteers and trainees in basic building skills. Electrical and plumbing works were sub-contracted.

This seems to have been a rewarding process for everyone involved. The method opens a door on an architectural philosophy which isn't about monumentality; trainees gained confidence and learnt skills (being prompt was high on Backes' agenda) which opened another door labelled 'anything is possible' ... as long as you turn up on time!

For details of other current schemes, contact The Walter Segal Self-Build Trust, 57 Chalton Street, London NW1 (0171–388 9582).

ADDRESS 160 Mill Lane, London NW6 [5H 43]
CLIENT Camden Society for People with Learning Difficulties (CSMH)
STRUCTURAL ENGINEER Trigram Partnership
CONTRACT VALUE £70, 400 (excluding architect's and engineer's fees)
SIZE 169 square metres
TUBE Kilburn – Jubilee Line
ACCESS open (but introduce yourself to whoever is around when you arrive)

Simon Yauner Architects 1992

Lisson Grove and Hampstead

Lisson Grove and Hampstead

Simon Yauner Architects 1992

City of London

Goldman Sachs UK Headquarters

A large-scale office building initiated in 1987 at the height of the building boom and executed through the economic decline of the last three years. It is appropriate that a US firm should receive this commission, a sign of the impact that American fast-track construction methods had on London in the 1980s. In true New York style, the building occupies a significant part of the skyline along Fleet Street, but in sympathy with the London infrastructure it goes almost unnoticed as you walk along the street (it sits behind the Daily Telegraph Building and is best viewed from Waterloo Bridge).

The interior detailing has the corporate glamour of the movie *Wall Street*, a cathedral of immaculately finished stainless steel and glass, marble and granite floors – all terrifically breathtaking and intimidating in its symmetry and scale. The exterior is clad in grey stone, with flush tall windows corresponding to the height of surrounding buildings and square ones above, giving the building its two identities when viewed from varying distances. Its presence is almost Speerian. It is hard not to notice the similarity of the south-facing façade with Farrell's nearby river frontage at Charing Cross.

ADDRESS Peterborough Court, 133 Fleet Street, London EC4 [7J 61]
CLIENT Goldman Sachs Company
STRUCTURAL ENGINEER Ove Arup & Partners
ASSOCIATED ARCHITECTS epr architects limited
SIZE 45,000 square metres
TUBE Aldwych – Piccadilly Line, then view from Waterloo Bridge
BUS 1, 4, 6, 11, 13, 15, 15B, X15, 68, X68, 77A, 168, 171, 171A, 176, 188, 196, 501, 502, 505, 513 to the Strand
ACCESS none

City of London

Kohn Pederson Fox Associates 1991

The Cochrane Theatre

Nigerian-born architect Abiodun Odedina, a partner in the young practice Robinson Thorne Architects, organised the transformation of the old faceless 1960s' Cochrane Theatre to provide the new home for the black theatre company, Talawa. The goal, which determined the way that the remodelling developed, was to give a cultural identity to Talawa whilst providing a pleasant working atmosphere and appropriate environment for its culturally mixed audiences. The existing building was a jumble of unused spaces with cramped bar and foyer areas, so the architects linked these together to form a long bar and open seating area on the first floor and wrapped them in a glass curve which bulges out to form a new front to the building. The glazing also encompasses part of the Arts and Crafts classical façade of Central St Martin's Art School next door.

Inside, the walls and existing structural elements have been painted bold colours to be read as coherent sculptural parts against the chaos of Theobalds Road outside. The auditorium is reached through a carved door which depicts Ogun, the Yoruba guardian of creativity. Students from the art school use the theatre space for rehearsals during the day so this remodelling project has provided a dynamic new public space and provides a home for the only black theatre company in Britain staging original productions in its own building.

ADDRESS Southampton Row, London WC1 [5J 61]
CLIENT Talawa Theatre Company and The London Institute
CONTRACT VALUE £400,000
TUBE Holborn – Central, Piccadilly Lines
BUS 7, 8, 19, 22B, 25, 30, 38, 55, 68, 168, 171, 188, 196, 501, 505 to High Holborn
ACCESS open

City of London

Robinson Thorne Architects 1991

Robinson Thorne Architects 1991

ITN Headquarters

The new headquarters building for Independent Television News is easily identifiable along a street of office developments as the work of Foster Associates because of the huge expanse of glass discreetly fixed onto the undisguised skeleton of the building.

The layered entrance is an impressive feature. Set back from the pavement, it is defined by a glass screen containing the tallest revolving doors in Europe. This screen cuts diagonally behind structural, thin, round columns. If you only manage to get as far as the reception area this will be enough to give you a sense of the quality of space in the rest of the building – vast and light, making the black leather Le Corbusier chairs look like doll's-house furniture. From here one has a view into the naturally lit atrium beyond, through tall glass partitions – small gaps in between each sheet prevent feelings of separation from the other spaces. The walkways that link either side of the gap, forming meeting points for employees, become silhouetted against the luminous glow which filters through the translucent glass on the south end. The exposed, ribbed concrete floor slabs float in this light.

The site used to be occupied by *The Times* – ITN's studios are sited in the basement where printing presses once lived. The rest of the space has been designed so that the organization can expand or let out upper levels.

ADDRESS Gray's Inn Road, London WC1 [3K 61]
CLIENT Stanhope Properties plc and Independent Television News
STRUCTURAL ENGINEER Ove Arup & Partners
SIZE 37,000 square metres
TUBE Chancery Lane – Central Line
BUS 17, 45, 171A, 243 to Gray's Inn Road
ACCESS none

City of London

Foster Associates 1989

City of London

Foster Associates 1989

Ludgate

Ludgate is like a baby Broadgate, one sixth of the size and 30 per cent cheaper to build. Although from the same stable (Rosehaugh Stanhope Development), it is a more mature development than Broadgate. Having been conceived during the time of building mania in the mid 1980s (Broadgate was about building at speed), Ludgate has benefited from the necessity of trimming costs in the early 1990s. The buildings have become less ornate (less expensive tack) and more functional in plan and in appearance, making them easier to maintain. Costs were reduced by lowering floor-to-floor heights, reducing the thickness of external walls from 300 mm to 250 mm, and keeping central cores as small as possible.

The 1.5-km-long site straddles railway tracks going into Blackfriars. Trains were stopped for 17 days, in which time a viaduct was partly dismantled, a bridge was removed, the train tracks were realigned and a huge raft was constructed over the tracks to form the base of the development. All the buildings rest on springs which attenuate the vibrations from the underground trains much more than the usual Neoprene pads, making the movements less jarring and the buildings effectively bouncy! The courtyard between the buildings is occupied by a painted steel sculpture by Bruce McLean.

This project was an exercise in how to begin seriously cutting building costs and to work with less staff. There was even a pilot scheme to challenge the ritual of the British workman's tea break. Bovis, the construction managers, encouraged workers to take breaks at flexible times in 'satellite' canteens on site. To avoid a complete shutdown at 9.00 when all the workers went off to the café for breakfast, it was suggested that breakfast be served on site in order to start work at 8.00, thus keeping the employees at work 20 per cent longer each day. Goodness knows what effect this precedent would have had on British greasy-spoon culture.

City of London

Skidmore, Owings & Merrill, Inc. 1992

City of London

Skidmore, Owings & Merrill, Inc. 1992

Individual buildings:

1 Ludgate Place
Skidmore, Owings & Merrill, Inc. 1992
Steel frame, panelised wall system of steel fins and aluminium spandrels.

10 Ludgate Place
Skidmore, Owings & Merrill, Inc. 1992
Steel frame with unitised system of aluminium and granite fins.

100 Ludgate Hill
Skidmore, Owings & Merrill, Inc. 1992
Reinforced concrete structure, precast concrete panelised system with limestone.

100 New Bridge Street
Renton Howard Wood Levin 1992
Steel frame with precast concrete cladding.

ADDRESS Ludgate Hill, London EC4 [6B 62]
CLIENT Rosehaugh Stanhope Development plc
in conjunction with British Rail Property Board
TOTAL CONTRACT VALUE £400 million
SIZE 76,250 square metres
TUBE Blackfriars – District, Circle Lines
BUS 9, 11, 45, 59, 76, 172, 502, 513
to Ludgate Circus
ACCESS none

Skidmore, Owings & Merrill, Inc. 1992

City House

CZWG are well known for creating bold imagery, taking themes from the site and the personality of the occupant and reflecting these in the plans and the use of materials. The basic construction here is straightforward and economica: brick with standard concrete floors. The external themes seem to be a mixture of Scottish baronial (cast concrete log lintels), French château (part mansard roof) and screens like the sails of a boat.

Inside there are plain plaster walls (which get lighter as you progress up the four levels) and ceilings are left bare to expose floor slabs. The top-floor studio is lined with unpainted chipboard which has a glowing natural colour and provides insulation. What appears to be a basic rectangular shell has then been elaborated by the internal plan which is based around a circular geometry, dictated by a curving staircase which runs around the perimeter. This arrangement creates a large sweeping space (the bedroom on the first floor), or a space like a castle ante-chamber for the dining room leading onto the main living room on the second floor.

The most-publicized aspect of the house must be the kitchen where the wall surfaces reveal their stud partitioning – a pioneering example of the distressed look, a theme which cropped up in many interior landmarks of the 1980s. With a terrace outside the studio on the top floor, it goes to show that in England, every media person's home could be not only their castle, but their playground too.

ADDRESS Britton Street, Smithfield, London EC1 [4B 62]
SIZE 350 square metres
TUBE Farringdon – Circle, Metropolitan Lines
BUS 55, 63, 243 to Farringdon Road
ACCESS none

City of London

CZWG Architects 1986–1988

CZWG Architects 1986–1988

Alban Gate

The redevelopment of Lee House is a major urban-design project which is intended to serve as the gateway to the City of London. Buildings along London Wall have been redeveloped and now provide space for housing, shops and a square. Almost 35,000 square metres of office space have been accommodated in an air-rights block spanning the road intersection of London Wall and Wood Street and in the new Lee House which is on the site of the old structure, forming one complete office building.

The design also incorporates a smaller office, retail and accommodation West Wing, and has involved the relandscaping of Monkwell Square to provide a 'traditional London square', and the construction of two basement-level car parks.

Severe granite- and glass-clad towers culminate in a glass vault at roof level – this combination of materials was used in order to break up the solidity of the mass, the solid areas relating to office space and the glazed areas relating to the internal atria. Major structural elements, such as truss beams, cross bracing and the heavy glazing system are incorporated into the façades. There is also a cosmetic attempt to adopt the scale of surrounding buildings by using a different-coloured granite lower down on the façades. An unremarkable office block and bland visual hurdle this development is, a 'gateway' it is not.

ADDRESS 125 London Wall, London EC2 [5C 62]
CLIENT MEPC
CONTRACT VALUE £115 million
SIZE 60,400 square metres
TUBE Barbican or Moorgate – District, Circle Lines
BUS 4, 9, 11, 21, 43, 76, 133, 141, 172, 214, 502 to London Wall
access none

City of London

Terry Farrell & Company 1987–1992

Minster Court

The new seat of the London Underwriting Centre, Minster Court, has been dubbed 'Munster Court', making a more-than-suitable set for the 1960s' spoof horror television series. This gothic chocolate cake comprises three steel-framed blocks merged into one by a curtain wall, the surface of which constantly changes direction forming icing peaks and mock buttresses. The granite panels are 7.5 metres wide by a full storey high and were transported on specially adapted trucks that could cope with their size. The ground floor slab was made considerably more substantial so that vehicles could drive into the centre of the building during construction, therefore speeding up the process. Toilet pods were designed by Mitsubishi.

There is 50 per cent more space here than in the Lloyd's Building, arranged around a central atrium. Horrifyingly, in August 1991 one of the three buildings went up in smoke, causing £120 million worth of damage. The fire started at the base of the atrium then spread rapidly; the escalators were wrapped in sterling board which encouraged the fire considerably. The accident was blamed on debris left around the site, thus prompting attention towards installation of fire protection earlier in the construction process.

ADDRESS Mark Lane, London EC3 [7E 62]
CLIENT Prudential Portfolio Managers
CONTRACT VALUE £178 million
SIZE 59,000 square metres
TUBE Tower Hill – District, Circle Lines
BUS 15, 25, 100 to Tower Hill
ACCESS none

GMW Partnership 1988–1991

City of London

GMW Partnership 1988–1991

1 America Square

This, the last in a spate of so-called 'air-rights' buildings, occupies the space above Fenchurch Street Station (another example of this building type can be seen at Charing Cross Station). It envelopes a stretch of the Roman London Wall, now a feature of the lower ground floor.

This building is a lesson in how to make a mock-1930s' Manhattan office block while the process of building was also a lesson in construction management. When the project began it was beset with delays: a steel strike just as the frame was near completion, then high winds tampered with schedules. The job was handed over to a Japanese firm to rework a schedule to ensure that it would be completed on time. This was primarily achieved by completely reorganizing the site, with one site office for direct communication between all workers instead of the usual scattered sources of information which inevitably slow down the building process.

The result is just a more glamorous version of so many office buildings of this era, a glitzy display of three shades of granite, polished stainless-steel canopies and light fixtures and white marble floors. Everything you would expect from prime office space but with a hint of movie nostalgia to suit the tastes of this client.

ADDRESS 1 America Square, London EC3 [7F 63]
CLIENT Central and City Developers
SIZE 19,350 square metres
TUBE Tower Hill – District, Circle Lines
BUS 15, 25, 100 to Tower Hill
ACCESS none

City of London

Renton Howard Wood Levin 1988

City of London

Renton Howard Wood Levin 1988

Lloyd's of London Insurance Market and Offices

This is not a tower block – it is rarely perceived as a whole at any one time. More like a vertical street, one sees bits of gleaming stainless steel, or electric-blue light at night, patched onto the sober City landscape. Its close proximity to other buildings allows it physically to penetrate the surroundings. The unusual configuration is a result of the building's location within the irregular medieval street pattern and the dominant philosophy that the building should appear to be assembled from a 'kit of parts'.

The main structure is remarkably simple in plan: a stack of 'O' ring floors (varying in level from six to twelve storeys) carried on central concrete columns and braced external columns creating a support for the vast steel tubular lattice framework of the 70-metre-high atrium. Six precast concrete satellite service towers cling, structurally independent, to the exterior of the main frame; the lavatory modules plugged into the sides can feasibly be replaced. The tower is surmounted by five stunning electric-blue cranes. All of the structural details are in full view, giving you the viewer an understanding of how the building is supported and braced.

Inside, the atmosphere is awesomely cathedral-like. The whole point of the Lloyd's building is to house one of the world's most famous financial institutions, so the focus for the activities taking place is on the underwriting room (the Room) on the ground floor and first three mezzanine levels. 'Boxes' are provided on each floor which are flexible work terminals containing storage units, work tops, VDUs, telephones, etc., to be rented by the underwriters. The boxes were developed as kits by Tecno. This type of open-plan, flexible, fully-serviced space is called an 'omniplatz'. Light pours down into the canyon-like atrium space and additional light comes from large fittings, which also act as air extrac-

Richard Rogers Partnership 1978–1986

City of London

Richard Rogers Partnership 1978–1986

tors, set into the ceiling. The triple-glazed external cladding skin acts as an air duct from ceiling to floor.

With enough stainless steel to make 20,000 sinks, ducting and pipes that could stretch from London to Brighton, floor space to cover seven football pitches, and unique and thorough detailing (many parts performing more than one task) this building is functionally and aesthetically a living and breathing machine.

ADDRESS Lime Street, London EC3 [7E 62]
CLIENT Corporation of Lloyd's of London
STRUCTURAL ENGINEER Ove Arup & Partners
CONTRACT VALUE £169 million
SIZE 47,000 square metres
TUBE Monument – District and Circle Lines
BUS 15, 25, 40, 100 to Fenchurch Street
ACCESS only by booking in advance;
telephone 0171-623 7100

City of London

Richard Rogers Partnership 1978–1986

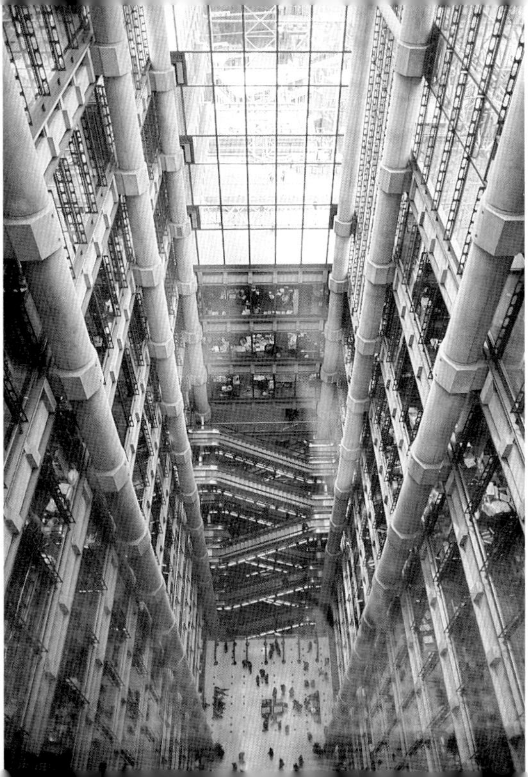

54 Lombard Street

You thought you had seen the last of the wedding-cake office developments of the early 1980s but here is one to top them all – with a three-tiered mass. The surprise, however, is that here the form of the metal-faced tower seems to be trying to blend in with its adolescent neighbour (in architectural years) rather than leafing through the antique dictionary for stylistic references. The resemblance to the lofty arched atrium at the summit of the nearby Lloyd's Building is remarkable. Further down the elevation, at street level, the building relaxes back into a weighty, grey granite-clad façade incorporating some of the classical details of the Victorian and Edwardian buildings adjoining. Inside there are 18 glorious floors of office space.

City of London

ADDRESS 54 Lombard Street, London EC3 [6D 62]
CLIENT Barclays Property Holdings
SIZE 41,300 square metres
TUBE Bank – Northern and Central Lines
BUS 15, 17, 25 to Bank
ACCESS none

GMW Partnership 1993

City of London

GMW Partnership 1993

Billingsgate Securities Market

The site occupies what was Billingsgate Fish Market, a Grade II listed building constructed in 1875 by Sir Horace Jones (who also designed Tower Bridge), facing onto the River Thames. Fish had been sold here since medieval times until, in 1982, the market was moved out to the West India Docks, along with so many other City-based industries, like the newspapers. Sir Horace Jones's Billingsgate is a hall flanked by aisles on the north and south sides. It is built of yellow London stock bricks with Portland stone dressings and granite plinths on a solid 15-metre-deep foundation. Inside, the main feature is the large hall divided in the centre by the Haddock Gallery.

The first proposal for the redevelopment of Billingsgate, once it had become vacant, was by Chrysalis Architects (a short-lived practice comprising Alan Stanton, Ian Ritchie and Mike Davies). Their scheme was for a restaurant and shopping complex. In 1985 Citicorp bought the site in order to develop it as a new headquarters with a dealing floor and offices to be equipped with the latest technology. The Richard Rogers Partnership was their architect.

The aim was to restore the building faithfully, while making new elements structurally and visually independent. The main hall has been converted into the single largest dealing floor in the City of London (9400 square metres). Heat from the projected 1500 computer terminals was to be extracted through ducts in a raised floor, which means that the spectacular 20-metre span of glazed roof with lattice girders is uninterrupted. The original glazing has been replaced with prismatic glass to prevent glare on the VDU units, projecting a calm, even light. The arcaded street frontage has been glazed in plate glass to eliminate traffic noise and the arcaded south-facing river frontage is shielded from the sun by light-sensitive Venetian blinds. An extra 3300 square metres of

Richard Rogers Partnership 1985–1988

space has been added with new mezzanine floors, suspended beneath the Haddock Gallery and around the aisles. They are free-standing structures which can be moved at any time. The 8-metre-high, groined vaulted basement, once used for refrigeration of the fish, now has a new mezzanine level and a restaurant space.

It is an all-too-familiar story: once the project had been completed the financial crash that hit the City in 1987 left the banks feeling nervous, so to this day Billingsgate remains empty. The architects have done a superb job in renovating a stunning Victorian building and integrating modern technology without descending to mimicry. However, it is a tragedy that public access is forbidden (except along the new river frontage). A prime site and an integral part of the City of London has been snatched out of public hands to feed an insatiable private appetite. Now that Citibank has so kindly financed the desperately needed restoration, perhaps the building can be put to more imaginative use.

ADDRESS Lower Thames Street, London EC3 [7E 62]
CLIENT Citibank/Citicorp
STRUCTURAL ENGINEER Ove Arup & Partners
CONTRACT VALUE £20 million
SIZE 11,200 square metres
TUBE Monument – District, Circle Lines
BUS 15, 25, 100 to Monument
ACCESS none

City of London

Richard Rogers Partnership 1985–1988

Tower Bridge Visitors' Facilities

The building forms an entrance to a new exhibition which was redesigned in 1994 to commemorate the centenary of the construction of Tower Bridge. Completion of the entrance pavilion had to coincide with the opening of the exhibition. In order to speed things along a design and build contract was employed before Michael Squire Associates were appointed to complete the job and to proceed with the design and construction of a new restaurant on the south side of the bridge.

The visitors' pavilion provides an enclosure for a ticket office and staff facilities. The main structure consists of two central beams which carry lateral beams cantilevered to the perimeter then held down with tie rods. The orientation of the building and its glazed walls take full advantage of the river views as it wraps itself around the existing curved parapet wall. Terrazzo panels replace glass to form an enclosure on the south side for staff quarters.

The new structure has adopted an appearance more akin to the fine tracery which decorates the bridge than to its heavy granite piers. A contemporary frill.

ADDRESS north side of Tower Bridge [F1 79]
CLIENT Corporation of London
CONTRACT VALUE £230,000
TUBE Tower Hill – District and Circle Lines
BUS 25, 42, 78, P11 to north or south side of Tower Bridge
ACCESS open 10.00–17.15, seven days a week

City of London

Michael Squire Associates 1993

Michael Squire Associates 1993

Bracken House

The original Bracken House was the Grade II listed home of the *Financial Times* (hence the pink stone), built by Sir Albert Richardson in 1959. The dispersal of the newspaper industry to developing areas such as Docklands throughout the 1980s left many valuable sites in the City empty, to be converted into London bases for American and Japanese merchant banks. The old *FT* building had two office block wings linked by an unspectacular octagonal printworks in the centre. It was this central part that Hopkins demolished and re-addressed.

A new oval plan has been sandwiched between the old wings. None of the old building was at right angles with the site; the wings are not aligned, whereas the Hopkins doughnut has been set parallel to Friday Street so that it bulges out as if being squeezed in a clamp. The plan is centred on a rectangular atrium. It contains lifts and glass pavement brick walkways all the way around to allow light to filter into the heart of the office floors. The four corners are marked by hollow, wedge-shaped columns which contain services. The six floors are concrete on metal decking, the thickness being kept to a minimum to reduce the total height of the building in accordance with the St Paul's Cathedral height rules.

Each floor is open-plan with a 4-metre deep rim around the edge marked by secondary columns, to allow for any partitioning or private spaces. This rim is crucial to the nature of the façade. Hopkins's belief is that architectural form is based on structure. The brief here was that the façade be long-life, low maintenance and structural and to refer to the materials of the old building. Ground, load-bearing piers are of solid Hollington stone (sandstone used in Richardson's building). The bay window panels resting on huge three-armed brackets, also load-bearing, are made of gun-metal (bronze, zinc and lead), a structural material. In the event of a fire the floor beams in the 4-metre span act as cantilevers

Michael Hopkins & Partners 1989–1991

Michael Hopkins & Partners 1989–1991

so that no added fire protection was required, hence the exposed material on the outside. Ceiling fixing plates on the inside indicate where brackets connect the outside structure with the inside floor slabs.

Bracken House is technically very creative and materials have been tested beyond decorative roles, but on the face of it, it is heavy and rather dreary. Not only is it squeezed from the sides, but St. Paul's has squashed it with its big foot too.

ADDRESS 1 Friday Street, London EC4 [7C 62]
CLIENT Obayashi Europe BV: Harakazu Nakamua
STRUCTURAL ENGINEER Ove Arup & Partners
TUBE Mansion House – District, Circle Lines
BUS 9, 11, 15, 17, 76, 513 to Mansion House
ACCESS none

City of London

Michael Hopkins & Partners 1989–1991

Michael Hopkins & Partners 1989–1991

This is the commercial building debut of one of the most distinguished British architects. Sir Denys Lasdun's career is marked by such projects as the apartments at 26 St James's Place, SW1 (1958), the Royal College of Physicians near Regent's Park (early 1960s) and the National Theatre on the South Bank (1969). These works are grounded by a sense of social responsibility; designed at a time when a building opportunity offered the potential for architectural experimentation with the will to enhance society. Now architects are at the mercy of construction techniques and predatory clients. Symbols borrowed from other eras pinned to steel frames replace responses to specific environmental problems.

Here the metaphor is 'the castle' (borrowed from the nearby Barbican and Lasdun's interest in C R Mackintosh), but unlike other fortress-offices nearby (with wretched granite walls and impervious mirrored glass) Milton Gate is a modest watery stronghold. A partially visible grid frame is veiled in blue-green glass, giving a semi-transparent and occasionally rippled effect. The double skin provides a space between the glass and frame for maintenance walkways and reduces solar gain and heat loss. The interior is based around a central courtyard and moated elevator tower with walkways overhead linking the offices around the sides. Poor materials let the side down – the central space is cloaked in a grey panelled pallor. Sir Denys deserves better than this.

ADDRESS Chiswell Street, London EC2 [5D 62]
CLIENT Land Securities
SIZE 19,700 square metres
TUBE Barbican – District and Circle Lines (through Beech Street tunnel)
BUS 4, 56, 172 to the Barbican
ACCESS none

Denys Lasdun Peter Softley & Associates 1990

Denys Lasdun Peter Softley & Associates 1990

Liverpool Street to Stansted

Liverpool Street Station

The first train arrived at Liverpool Street Station in 1875. The original L-shaped plan was determined by the two types of mainline termini. There was one long platform for the long-distance trains with its ticket offices alongside, and six short platforms for suburban trains accessible from the main concourse. The roof was built in four spans, two over the lines flanked by aisles. In 1894 eight more suburban train platforms were built to the east of the original lines, but no concourse accompanied them so they were tentatively linked by a footbridge. The roof was also extended to make a transept over the new station. Mass planning confusion ensued with the addition of the Underground stations.

The general plan for new engineering work on the station involved extending a section of the roof span on the south-west side to make a wider concourse with the addition of a second transept along this southern end providing two new entrances. The shed containing the eight platforms added in 1894 has been covered by the Bishopsgate development. The north end, where open tracks once lay, is now covered with a raft structure holding Exchange House and a public square, from which you have the most superb view of the inside of the train shed and its wrought-iron roof. The contract also involved the building of a new Underground ticket hall and the relocation of the underground Post Office delivery chutes.

Inside, the cast-iron acanthus-leaf capitals supporting the roof structure have been fully restored. The design contract covered all new interventions, such as the raised, covered walkway which accommodates shops and cafés and bisects the main concourse, obscuring a view of the tracks as you enter from Liverpool Street. The design of the new parts was intended to be thoroughly modern to contrast with the Victorian brick shed. Admirably, there has been no attempt to mimic old styles but

Architecture & Design Group, British Rail 1985–1991

Architecture & Design Group, British Rail 1985–1991

the new parts are crude, adopting abstract shapes, and the structural elements are clumsy.

There are two new entrances, one on Bishopsgate, a bizarre composition of a small square covered by a shopping-mall-type canopy flanked by two red-brick Italianate towers. These towers are repeated at the Liverpool Street entrance, but here the canopy is a piece of protruding trainshed roof, and a glass screen hangs between the towers like a portcullis ready to drop shut after the last train has departed for the night. Unfortunately, the illusion is abandoned as you will see a band of sliding glass doors along the bottom which secure the station at night.

Each of the additions seem to have been designed in isolation so there is a lack of overall coherence in the new scheme. However, the general circulation at plaform level has improved considerably and the link made between Broadgate and Bishopsgate is significant in interweaving public and private interests by way of a major railway terminus.

ADDRESS Liverpool Street/Bishopsgate, London EC2 [5E 62]
CLIENT Network South East, British Rail Board
STRUCTURAL ENGINEERS New Works Engineers, Network South East; YRM Anthony Hunt Associates; Frank Graham & Partners; De Leuw Chadwick Witham
CONTRACT VALUE £120 million
TUBE Liverpool Street – Central, Circle, Metropolitan Lines
BUS 9, 11, 141, 502 to Liverpool Street
ACCESS open

Architecture & Design Group, British Rail 1985–1991

Liverpool Street to Stansted

Architecture & Design Group, British Rail 1985–1991

Broadgate

The City of London is the home of a strong international commercial power. During the 1980s, Prime Minister Thatcher's government deregulated many financial activities to open up a new age of international electronic trading. Banks and brokers merged, and started to demand a new type of office space with large floorplates, floor-to-floor heights big enough to accommodate under-floor cabling, spaces which could be flexible and able to cope with 24-hour operations and suitable for employees working under highly stressful conditions. The demand was met between 1985 and 1991 by the addition of 4.5 million square metres of office space in central London. Broadgate provided some 334,450 square metres of this space, equal to the amount of space provided by five Empire State Buildings.

The site has for more than a century been a crossover point between the City and the influx of employees arriving at Liverpool Street Station. Globally, it sits between New York and Tokyo, providing a perfect base for foreign financiers.

Extensive research into client requirements revealed that North American office environments were admired: i.e. the face of the buildings should be extremely impressive, with big lobbies and atria, large open-plan office floors, and facilities that would enhance the lives of the employees, like outdoor spaces, restaurants, bars and a health club. All of these undertakings were achieved at Broadgate within the context of the medieval street plan and its listed buildings.

The whole scheme consists of 13 buildings and three squares, built in 14 phases. The first four phases were masterminded by Arup Associates. The plan was generated from the patterns of movement of people coming to the site from Liverpool Street Station. Each phase had to be built in 12 months, six years in all. The secret to this speedy building system was

Arup Associates, Skidmore, Owings & Merrill, Inc. 1984–1991

Arup Associates, Skidmore, Owings & Merrill, Inc. 1984–1991

the prefabrication of many building parts off site. Most of the buildings have a steel frame with metal deck floors and external cladding to accommodate anything from an auditorium to a trading floor. Complete units, such as toilet pods, liftshafts and plant rooms, and the granite cladding with heating services incorporated, were all prefabricated and slotted into the steel frame.

More than half of the site is built on a raft which spans the railway tracks of Liverpool Street Station. Specific parts of the buildings were made by specialist fabricators under direct contract with the client in order to avoid the administrative mayhem of contractors and subcontractors. The project involved 2200 people on site and 19,000 drawings per week, so keeping simple and direct lines of communication open was essential.

A general picture of each of the buildings is outlined in the following list, but there are some buildings and public spaces of particular interest.

Exchange House, by the Chicago firm Skidmore, Owings & Merrill, Inc., owes much to bridge technology, as its four parabolic arches span the railway tracks. They rest on eight piers which support the entire building. The steel-framed box which encloses the office floors hangs between the arches. It is the most expressive of all the Broadgate buildings because of the innovative technology used to create the container, articulated in the rawest of materials. The modern exterior hints at what is inside, equipped with the most advanced information technology in Britain. The square in front looks onto a superb, full-length view of the inside of the vaulted train sheds at Liverpool Street Station.

Also notable is Broadgate Square, by Arup Associates, with its circular ice rink in the centre surrounded by tiered terraces, like an amphitheatre, with cascading foliage. The terraces accommodate restaurants, bars and

Arup Associates, Skidmore, Owings & Merrill, Inc. 1984–1991

Arup Associates, Skidmore, Owings & Merrill, Inc. 1984–1991

shops behind which are the glass and granite façades of the office buildings. The square provides the desired public recreation area, but the surrounding buildings are faceless, making it seem an abrupt transition within the scheme, only fully animated at brief intervals in the day or at certain times of year. People seem to be forced to the place out of necessity rather than being drawn to it.

Helping to redeem the generally feeble architecture is the contribution of the many well-known contemporary artists who were commissioned to make work especially for the site. The vast steel sheets that make up 'Fulcrum' by Richard Serra rest tentatively against each other at the entrance to Broadgate Square, forming an integral part of the landscape. 'Leaping Hare on Crescent and Bell' by Barry Flanagan sits in the square. Inside 100 Liverpool Street just some of the work includes a bronze horse, also by Flanagan, a terrazzo reception desk and mural by Bruce McLean, and prints by Patrick Caulfield.

ADDRESS Broadgate, London EC2 [5E 62]
CLIENT Rosehaugh Stanhope Development plc in conjunction with British Rail Property Board
CONSTRUCTION MANAGEMENT Bovis and Schal
SIZE 3.6 hectares
TUBE Liverpool Street – Central, Circle, Metropolitan Lines
BUS 9, 11, 141, 502 to Liverpool Street
ACCESS public spaces are open

Arup Associates, Skidmore, Owings & Merrill, Inc. 1984–1991

Arup Associates, Skidmore, Owings & Merrill, Inc. 1984–1991

Tottenham Hale Station

Built at a time when the national railway system is threatened by privatization, this represents all that is opposed to such a move by showing how the public and private sectors can co-ordinate and work successfully together in public design (British Rail, London Underground, London Buses and the British Airport Authority all meet and co-operate at this interchange). Tottenham Hale celebrates railway architecture without nostalgia by anticipating a relaxed and more glamorous way to travel. It forms part of the journey from the high-tech Stansted Airport into central London, creating a stylish impression for first-time visitors.

As in many of Alsop's buildings, the structure and imaginative use of materials are boldly evocative of the station's function. The main external feature, a gleaming curved aluminium skin with portholes, looks like the side of an aeroplane or an emerging submarine and contains a buffet, waiting room and lavatories. Above this, integrated into the white steel and glass framework that spans the tracks, is a 53-metre painting by Bruce McLean on enamelled steel panels – a rare example of art which is an essential part of the architecture and not a decorative afterthought.

On a suprisingly low budget, an important and unusual architectural gesture has been made, contributing not only to a new generation of building in London, but also to the identity of the local community.

ADDRESS Ferry Lane, London N17 [4G 31]
CLIENT British Rail Network South East
ENGINEER Felix J Samuely & Partners
CONTRACT VALUE £2.3 million
TUBE Tottenham Hale – Victoria Line
BR from Liverpool Street or Stansted
ACCESS open

Alsop Lyall & Störmer 1991

Liverpool Street to Stansted

Alsop Lyall & Störmer 1991

Stansted Airport

There has been a runway at Stansted since 1942. In 1953 Stansted was singled out as London's potential third airport. Forty years and several public inquiries, reports, and committees later, the new terminal was opened by HM The Queen. Foster Associates became involved in the project in 1981. During the long gaps while decisions were being made in Whitehall the time was used positively to develop a good relationship with the client.

The main design concept for the airport derived from Foster's own love of flying (he would travel to the site, stress-free, in his own helicopter) and the simplicity of early airport terminals. The open fields of Stansted invited a low, single-storey building with a roadside entrance and car park on one side and the runway and aeroplane satellites on the other.

Travellers by rail arrive underneath the building and are transported via an escalator or lifts directly into the main concourse. Check-in, shops, security areas and departure lounge are arranged in a linear fashion to avoid excessive signage and disorientation, with views out to the runway. A monorail shuttle whisks passengers to the adjacent satellite for boarding. This ease of passage was greatly informed by many hours spent in airports whilst the architects flew back and forth from Hong Kong during the construction of the Hong Kong & Shanghai Bank.

The vast open space of the main building is clearly articulated by the spectacular roof structure which floats more than 15 metres above our heads. A quilt of square domes is supported by a grid of 36 service trees. The white roof membrane (perforated steel trays and insulated Sarnafil PVC) filters light down onto the grey terrazzo floor and reflects light from inside. The domes also act as smoke reservoirs with extractor fans built into the top of each tree. Another significant achievement in the design of the roof is the syphonic draining system which allows drainpipes to

Liverpool Street to Stansted

Foster Associates 1985–1991

be laid horizontally. All air-conditioning, information and lighting services are contained in the roof support/service pods, leaving the concourse space completely free of pipes and ducts. Travellers and airport staff can see the sky, the 'planes and the fields through the glazed perimeter walls all around. Remarkably, a highly technical and structurally sophisticated enclosure exudes the qualities of a natural environment.

Interior detailing was never treated as a separate issue as far as the architects were concerned. Everything from carpets and seating to check-in desks has been dealt with obsessively, each item having been custom-made for this particular terminal. Even the white, fire-proof retail 'cabins' have been rigorously designed so that they disguise loud shop logos and unsightly trad brass fittings. Check-in desks are made from a kit of stainless steel and linoleum-covered plywood parts that can be rearranged easily as more airlines move to Stansted.

It is anticipated that 8 million passengers a year will pass through the terminal by the end of this century, and there will be space to accommodate 15 million in the future. I hope that the surrounding infrastructure, the road and rail links, provide the necessary back-up.

ADDRESS Stansted, Essex
CLIENT British Airport Authority/Stansted Airport Limited
STRUCTURAL ENGINEER Ove Arup & Partners
CONTRACT VALUE £400 million
SIZE main terminal is 39,000 square metres
BR Stansted is approximately 40 minutes from Liverpool Street or Tottenham Hale
ROAD just off M11
ACCESS open

Foster Associates 1985–1991

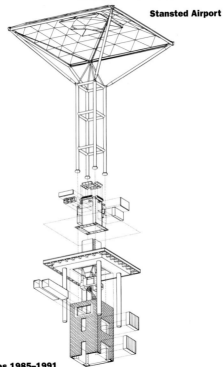

Foster Associates 1985–1991

Stepney to Wapping

Playground Canopy, St Anne's Infant School

This project was initiated by the BBC as part of a television series called *Public Property*, to be screened in 1996. Architects and designers were invited to make new interventions in neglected public areas. The tensile membrane structure rises in two peaks supported by telegraph poles inside and capped with metal cones outside, then swoops down to a low curved arch to form the mouth of the canopy. The landscaped floor plan beneath is built up to make an auditorium shape from stepped levels of hard-core covered in a spongy finish and edged in telegraph poles.

The outdoor classroom breaks new ground in the world of tensile-membrane structures in several ways. In particular, the tension rods have been lifted up to above ground level so that children do not trip on them; gravel around the bases of the posts discourages running. The caps act as a ventilators at the top of the canopy, and it is the first time that coloured shapes have been cut into tensional fabric. Colours are used to highlight tension points and blue ridges act as gutters.

The canopy is a joyful and innovative creation which sits menacingly beside uninspiring classroom huts. For this particular firm of architects it was the first time they had designed a tensile membrane structure, so it has been an adventure for everyone.

ADDRESS Hunton Street, London E1 [5G 63]
CLIENT St Anne's School
STRUCTURAL ENGINEER YRM Anthony Hunt Associates: Hanif Kara
TUBE Whitechapel – District, Hammersmith & City Lines
BUS 25, 253 to Whitechapel
ACCESS view from the street or inside by prior appointment only

McCormac Jamieson Prichard 1994

McCormac Jamieson Prichard 1994

Swanlea Secondary School

This is the first new secondary school to be built in London in the last ten years. It is designed to accommodate 1050 pupils, with meeting rooms for use outside school hours. More significantly, the layout and size of the classrooms and communication between them has been informed by the demands of the national curriculum (set out by the Conservative government in 1990), making it the first school of this kind. The building has created a new focus and social centre for a community which is culturally rich but economically run-down.

The plan is focused around a central covered street, or mall, lined by London stock brick buildings which in turn surround a series of courtyards and gardens on the south side of the mall and a car park on the north side. The dramatic curved glass sweep of the mall roof greets you on Brady Street and draws you into the heart of the building; an avenue of curved, tapered columns bowing like trees in the wind, restrained by clusters of diagonal struts which support the glazing. The method of passive solar-energy recovery means that during winter the mall acts as a heat source for the whole building. The glazed roof is made up of Okasolar Glass panels (a very specialised glass made up of prismatic strips that reflect the high summer sun and let in low winter sun), providing a much cheaper and more efficient alternative to blinds. During the summer the mall is ventilated at a high level, creating cross-ventilation vertically through the space, without the expense and dubious environmental impact of air-conditioning. Classrooms have shop windows fronting the mall so that work can be presented to the school community, each one making maximum use of natural light, heat and ventilation. This seems to be a tremendous success although many of the classrooms may not prove to be adaptable enough given the constant change in national curriculum requirements.

Percy Thomas Partnership/Hampshire County Architects 1991–1993

Percy Thomas Partnership/Hampshire County Architects 1991–1993

The gardens are outdoor classrooms: one is an ecological garden, another is an exhibition courtyard. Eerily marking the south-west corner of the site is the caretaker's house which is a stop-off point on the Jack the Ripper bus-tour, for this site was where the monster gruesomely finished off many of his victims.

The architects have responded to this semi-wasteland by making a positive statement which follows through from the imaginative overall plan and as far as possible in the details, within a very tight budget.

ADDRESS Brady Street, London E1 [4H 63]
CLIENT London Borough of Tower Hamlets Education Department
STRUCTURAL ENGINEER YRM Anthony Hunt Associates
CONTRACT VALUE £9.2 million
SIZE 10,500 square metres
TUBE Whitechapel – District and Metropolitan Lines
BUS 25, 253 to Whitechapel
ACCESS limited

Percy Thomas Partnership/Hampshire County Architects 1991–1993

Stepney to Wapping

Percy Thomas Partnership/Hampshire County Architects 1991–1993

Queen Mary College Library

Twenty-five years on and the British Library is still not open to the public. However, at Queen Mary College the very same architect is at work, applying 30 years experience of the genre to this modest university library. Firmly rooted in the Functionalist tradition, the library is designed on the basis of a thorough understanding of the activities and their characteristics. As in any building there are many functions. The project architect, M J Long, has referred to a paper written with Peter Carolin in 1974 ('Briefing Guide for Libraries'), where they state that the building should derive its origins from a set of needs and create an intelligible spatial order to resolve those needs. This means concentrating on 'balancing the requirements of different areas (reading, book stacks and staff) in order to develop an effective building'. Flexibility is a typical feature of most libraries which tends to imply a universal space (often resulting in a waste of energy and creating redundant spaces). The client was adamant that the library should be flexible so this was addressed in terms of the architect's philosophy.

The result is a cross section and bay plan, the junctions accommodating an overlap of activities. All the readers are seated around the perimeter, benefitting from natural light and trunking for computer terminals. Perimeter seating allows mechanical ventilation rather than air conditioning pumped into the centre of the building. A concrete frame is infilled with fair-faced blockwork inside, some columns hidden amongst the book stacks, others standing free and protected from rogue book trolleys by strips of maple (matching the desks). The specially designed lighting system is suspended from the troughed metal decking ceiling, creating an illusion of different ceiling heights, without the monotony of a suspended ceiling. Materials are robust and low-maintenance, if a little cheerless.

The precise organisation of activities has meant that the main staircase

Colin St John Wilson & Partners 1986–1988

Colin St John Wilson & Partners 1986–1988

occupies a generous space with views through to the library and onto the Mile End Road.

The external brick skin has an entirely different feel. The entrance courtyard on the east side is like the corner of a brick room, with thin white lines to define the edges. The ground is outlined by a paving grid which echoes the internal concrete frame grid. The brick is not of exceptional quality and the seemingly haphazard arrangment of windows in heavy frames distracts from a potentially strong frontage with its elegantly thin white cornice line. The rear façade, overlooking the cemetery, has a more uniform window pattern which is more satisfying. Interior details (furniture) lack a certain sophistication, but the library has a sturdy confidence unaffected by current preoccupations with style, which benefits the overall performance of the building.

ADDRESS Mile End Road, London E1 [5J 63]
CLIENT The Governing Body of Queen Mary College (University of London)
STRUCTURAL ENGINEER Ove Arup & Partners
CONTRACT VALUE £3,257,530
SIZE 6830 square metres in total
TUBE Stepney Green – District Line; Mile End – District and Central Lines
BUS 25, 106 to Mile End Road
ACCESS open

Colin St John Wilson & Partners 1986–1988

Stepney to Wapping

Colin St John Wilson & Partners 1986–1988

Tobacco Dock

This project comprised the restoration and conversion of a stunning Grade 1 listed tobacco warehouse into a shopping mall. The six vast sheds were built in 1806 by Daniel Alexander, principal surveyor of the London Dock Company. It was a modern structure in its day, built of cast iron and timber elements slotted together and held in place by the weight of the roof timbers. The brick-vaulted basement (the largest in the Docklands) held wine and spirits, tobacco was stored on the first floor. In the 1860s, tobacco was replaced by wool and skins from Australia, New Zealand and the Falkland Islands, and the first floor became known as the Skin Floor.

Much of the main structure was still intact despite bomb damage, but whole bays have been immaculately reconstructed, matching bricks, pine trusses and slate from the same Welsh quarry that Alexander had used. Every sixth cast-iron column is hollow, allowing rainwater to filter through the building and keep the original pine piles moist.

The current plan, being proposed by Gerald Ratner of high-street jewellery notoriety, is to convert the mall into a factory-outlet centre – a new retail trend providing cut-price designer goods, adopted from the USA.

ADDRESS Pennington Street, London E1 [7H 63]
CLIENT Brian Jackson & Lawrence Cohen Developers
CONTRACT VALUE £30 million
SIZE 16,260 square metres
TUBE Tower Hill – District, Circle Lines
BUS X15, 100 to The Highway
ACCESS open

Stepney to Wapping

Terry Farrell & Company 1987

Roy Square

This housing scheme is reminiscent of the schemes of the 1930s, arranging blocks of apartments around a central garden, creating a feeling of solidarity between the residents. There is the provision of space for shops and workshops at street level so that the basic needs of the residents can be catered for. (Dolphin Square in Pimlico is an early example of this type of housing plan. It has its own arcade of shops, a swimming pool and bars all within its defensible red brick walls.)

At Roy Square, the architect refers to the four blocks that make up the scheme as pavilions. They contain one-, two- and three-bedroom apartments and are linked by glazed bridges so that movement between the buildings is evident. The flat brick outer façades adopt their proportions from the surrounding Georgian architecture. Parking space is provided on the whole of the ground level so the garden is now at first-floor level and can be entered via some steps in the front elevation. The internal walls of the square are tiered so that as much light as possible is admitted into the garden. The pavilion-like quality is enhanced as the bottom tier has double-height glazing, taking on the appearance of long conservatories on the two long sides of the square. Each flat has access from, and a view of, the garden.

ADDRESS Narrow Street, London E3 [7A 64]
CLIENT Roy Properties Limited
STRUCTURAL ENGINEER Ove Arup & Partners
CONTRACT VALUE £7.6 million
SIZE 5000 square metres
DOCKLANDS LIGHT RAILWAY West Ferry
BUS P14, D1, 56, 86, 277, 278
ACCESS none

Ian Ritchie Architects 1988

Stepney to Wapping

Ian Ritchie Architects 1988

Stratford Bus Station

Like a tent in the desert, the bus station canopy welcomes you with flailing arms in the middle of the jammed one-way system that strangles a desolate suburban borough centre. It is the first in a series of new transport buildings planned for East London with the extension of the Jubilee Line underway and additions to the Docklands Light Railway. The roof canopy rises gracefully above the bedlam. It is made up of tensile fabric inverted umbrellas supported by a forest of steel columns set out on a grid to define the main waiting area. Each column contains channels for roof drainage and cable conduit for lighting. The inverted canopy form allows for double-decker buses to draw up to the stop beneath the shelter. Concourse services are encased in building blocks around the perimeter of the sheltered area and clad in graffiti-proof glass panels.

Despite clear sitelines throughout the concourse, absence of blind corners and enclosed spaces and generous glazed screens shielding the waiting rooms, the structure is still draped in an assortment of security paraphernalia such as video monitors and loud speakers.

Stepney to Wapping

ADDRESS Great Eastern Road, London E15 [7F 49]
CLIENT London Transport Buses
IN-HOUSE ARCHITECT Soji Abass
STRUCTURAL ENGINEER Anthony Hunt Associates
CONTRACT VALUE £2 million
DOCKLANDS LIGHT RAILWAY Stratford
TUBE Stratford – Central Line
ACCESS open

Stepney to Wapping

London Bus Transport Passenger Infrastructure 1994

20B Bisterne Avenue

The commission was to design housing for the London Borough of Waltham Forest that would achieve as dense an occupation of the site as possible without ignoring the scale of neighbouring buildings. The six family flats are arranged in an H plan around a communal stair which leads to upper flats and a view out across Waltham Forest. The kitchens in each flat overlook the central stair, creating an active social space, in the tradition of the tenement block which looked inward so that residents could watch out for one another. The plan allows for maximum enjoyment of sunlight and views to the south.

Construction is simple and cheap; block walls rendered and painted terracotta with cobalt blue on the inside walls – colours that Wickham is particularly fond of, and which appear in his other projects, intensifying the architectural experience.

ADDRESS 20B Bisterne Avenue, London E17 [3F 33]
CLIENT London Borough of Waltham Forest
STRUCTURAL ENGINEER YRM Anthony Hunt Associates
CONTRACT VALUE £375,000
SIZE six (two-bedroom) ground-floor flats
BR – Wood Street Walthamstow
ACCESS none

Wickham & Associates 1990

Wickham & Associates 1990

Bermondsey

Broadwall, Coin Street Housing

A site with a unique social and political history, in 1984 it was acquired for £1 million from the Greater London Council by a group of Waterloo and Southwark residents calling themselves the Coin Street Community Builders. A separate housing association, the Coin Street Secondary Housing Co-operative, was subsequently set up to get funding to develop individual housing sites. Once a scheme has been completed it is run by by its own co-operative, drawing tenants of mixed incomes and origins from Lambeth and Southwark. All adults are made members of the co-operative, responsible for setting and paying rents to the Secondary Housing Co-operative. Each tenant is sent on a 12-week training programme to develop the necessary managerial skills before moving in.

Because of the poor quality of the detailing in the initial schemes, subsequent housing has been commissioned on the basis of architectural competitions. Broadwall is the result of this policy.

The brief called for 25 dwellings including ten family houses with gardens, five two-bedroom three-person flats and ten one-bedroom two-person flats. A long terrace block is bounded on the east side by Broadwall providing direct access from the street and overlooks a new park on the west side. The layout of the scheme demonstrates a logical and effectively urban way to accommodate a mixture of people with different housing needs, addressing an ingrained scepticism towards building types such as tower blocks and busy streets.

The smaller flats for two people have been grouped together into a nine-storey tower at the north end of the site (the head); the flats may lack gardens but they do have a stunning view across the river. An elevator serves each floor individually for privacy and security. The neck and tail at the south end of the scheme is formed by two four-storey blocks for larger flats and the main body is a row of 11 three-storey family houses

Lifschutz Davidson Design 1995

Lifschutz Davidson Design 1995

Bermondsey

with direct access to the park.

All flats and houses have spacious kitchens and living rooms with a western outlook through full-height windows and balconies with enough room to sit out on. Bedrooms are located against the impenetrable brick wall on the street side.

A generous budget (80 per cent of which came from a Housing Corporation grant) allowed unusual attention to the quality of detailing which uses a wide (some might say extravagant) selection of materials. This should increase the project's longevity although the scheme is too expensive to serve as a model for other housing-association developments.

The site rests in the heart of a gold mine of approved architectural proposals: the Museum of Modern Art at Bankside Power Station by Herzog & de Meuron, the redevelopment at the South Bank by Richard Rogers, the reconstruction of the Globe Theatre and the mixed-use development of the OXO Tower (also by Lifschutz Davidson) – each one with the millenium in their sights. Once these projects are under way this barren area of Southwark will be enriched again with the provision of homes and the communal facilities to service them.

ADDRESS off Stamford Street, Southwark, London SE1 [1A 78]
CLIENT Coin Street Secondary Housing Co-operative
STRUCTURAL ENGINEER Buro Happold Consulting Engineers
SIZE 27 units on a 0.15-hectare site (the whole site is 5.3 hectares)
TUBE Waterloo – Northern and Bakerloo Lines
BUS 149, P11 to Stamford Street, between Waterloo and Blackfriars Bridge
ACCESS none to individual homes; the project can be seen from Stamford Street

Lifschutz Davidson Design 1995

Bermondsey

Lifschutz Davidson Design 1995

Butlers Wharf: Infrastructure

Conran Roche has been leading a comprehensive revitalization strategy to rebuild the infrastructure of Butlers Wharf and restore many of its 17 Grade II listed buildings. The site, acquired in 1984 for a mere £5 million, is within the London Bridge Conservation Area. The overall plan is to build up a community where people will want to live and work again, with leisure, retail, office, residential and industrial facilities.

At the beginning of this century the area was occupied by flour, corn and rice merchants. Everything and everybody was covered in a heavy dusting of white powder. Many of the warehouses were then used to store spices, and a few of these are still in operation and have continued life as normal as building works have been carried out around them – you can still smell the pungent aroma of cinnamon and nutmeg as you walk down Gainsford Street. There is a peculiarly ghostly air as much of the area lies derelict, evoking the atmosphere of Charles Dickens's *Oliver Twist*. It makes the place infinitely more enticing as there are still bits to explore.

The infrastructure includes the pedestrianization of Shad Thames and Lafone Street, refurbishment of existing streets to increase pavement widths, and upgrading of street services, such as lighting. The quayside and river edge have been completely rejuvenated with York stone to provide a promenade and a pontoon to give access to the rather-too-infrequent riverbus service.

It does seem that a rigorous plan has been set out to integrate new activities into the rich but decaying building fabric. Diverse areas of society are already settling in – students from the London School of Economics live next to luxury apartments which sit next to deserted Victorian warehouses, a community nursery, workshops and the Design Museum. With the proposal for a 350-seat cinema on Curlew Street, this will definitely

Bermondsey

Conran Roche 1988–1990

Bermondsey

Conran Roche 1988–1990

be an area where people will want to hang around in future, particularly if more efficient transport links are implemented.

The Butlers Wharf Building is at the heart of the development and is described more fully on page 250. Other buildings in the development (all the work of Conran Roche) include Nutmeg House (Gainsford Street; the offices of the architects upstairs, a community nursery and shop on the ground floor), the Cardamon Building (Shad Thames; five Grade II listed warehouses rehabilitated as 64 residential units connected by bridges to the back of the Butlers Wharf Building), the Coriander Building (Gainsford Street; two Victorian warehouses converted to office space, now linked by a glazed service core), and Cinnamon Wharf (Shad Thames; a seven-storey warehouse converted into 66 flats).

ADDRESS Butlers Wharf, LONDON SE1 [2F 79]
CLIENT Butlers Wharf Limited
CONTRACT VALUE £6.5 million
SIZE 4.5-hectare site
TUBE Tower Hill – Circle and District Lines, walk over Tower Bridge
BUS 42, 47, 78, 188, P11 to south side of Tower Bridge
ACCESS open

Conran Roche 1988–1990

Bermondsey

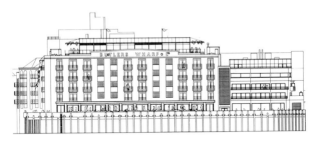

Conran Roche 1988–1990

The Butlers Wharf Building

This Grade II listed building, completed in 1874, is the most important on the site. The inside has been completely rebuilt using a reinforced-concrete frame, thus creating space for a new basement floor for parking. The discarded bricks were used to restore the façades, many of which were severely dilapidated. New pediments and cornices were constructed in glass-reinforced cement.

The building now accommodates 98 luxury apartments. The living rooms overlook the river through glazed doors which open onto new and uninteresting balconies. The ground floor is occupied by shops and restaurants, again created by Terence Conran. The Pont de la Tour restaurant and nearby delicatessen have a luxurious Parisian feel to them. The entire restaurant has a glass frontage overlooking the river. In the summer, café tables outside make use of the wide promenade.

The back of the building is linked across Shad Thames by cast-iron and timber bridges once used for transferring bags of wheat flour from one building to another, creating the 'canyon' street. The bridges now provide additional balcony space for some of the apartments. This street also reveals the backstage activities of the Pont de la Tour. Large windows provide passers-by with a clear view into the kitchens where anyone can stand for hours and watch the chefs preparing lobster and making fresh pasta.

ADDRESS Butlers Wharf, London SE1 [2F 79]
CLIENT Butlers Wharf Limited
TUBE Tower Hill – Circle and District Lines, walk over Tower Bridge
BUS 42, 47, 78, 188, P11 to south side of Tower Bridge
ACCESS none

Bermondsey

Conran Roche 1987–1989

Conran Roche 1987–1989

Design Museum

The Design Museum was set up by Terence Conran (founder of Habitat Stores and The Conran Shop) and Stephen Bayley to explain the function, appearance and marketing of consumer goods. The intention is to help to raise the awareness of design standards in everything from kettles to cars, from the earliest days of mass production. It also provides a resource to inform the work of the present-day design industry. It can be seen as a monument to the changing status of design during the Thatcher era. The objects in the museum are design classics which have now become cult objects – strangely contradictory.

The disused 1950's warehouse overlooking the River Thames has been reconstructed to accommodate a permanent Study Collection with limited reference material available at interactive computer terminals, a space for temporary exhibitions, a library, a lecture theatre and the Blueprint Café. The project started as a refurbishment but it proved cheaper to demolish and rebuild much of the original building because of a new VAT ruling on all construction except new building in the 1984 Budget.

The Study Collection is housed on the top floor in a double-height space, saturated in natural light which causes the neutral English oak and marble floors and white walls to glow. The temporary gallery is the usual white space that can be changed to exhibit anything from the corporate logos of Raymond Loewy to the furniture of Eileen Gray. Both the interior spaces were designed by Stanton Williams.

The Blueprint Café, designed by Terence Conran, is the only facility that really makes use of the original building and its prime location, by employing the layered frontage. The entrance, up a wide white stairwell, rather like the echoing approach to a swimming baths, leads customers into the open café area with its glass frontage and a terrace overlooking the Thames. The proximity of the water and the coolness of the space

Conran Roche 1987–1989

Bermondsey

Conran Roche 1987–1989

make you feel like you could be dining luxuriously on a cruise liner rather than on dry land.

The museum itself, once a red brick building, now rendered and painted white, undoubtedly pays tribute to the simplicity of the Modern Movement. The café, on the other hand, is a product of Conran's noble quest since the early 1980s to educate our ignorant British palates with Mediterranean cooking. However, given the situation, I think it would be more of an education to eat something that Mies van der Rohe or Mr. Olivetti might have had for lunch.

ADDRESS Shad Thames, London SE1 [2F 79]
CLIENT The Conran Foundation
CONTRACT VALUE £5.1 million
SIZE 3700 square metres gross
TUBE Tower Hill – Circle and District Lines, walk over Tower Bridge
BUSES 42, 47, 78, 188, P11 to south side of Tower Bridge
ACCESS 10.30–17.30, seven days a week

Bermondsey

Conran Roche 1987–1989

Conran Roche 1987–1989

London School of Economics Student Residence

This is a six-storey building with 280 student rooms served by four separate cores – each stairwell gives access to a pair of flats at each level. One flat comprises six single study bedrooms with built-in furniture and storage facilities – although they are rather cramped it was essential to make maximum use of the limited space. Each flat has a communal dining/living area with a balcony which faces south on to Gainsford Street. The new block could be mistaken for more luxurious apartments but the orange plastic chairs and piles of laundry that spew out onto the balconies give it that authentic hall of residence feel.

It is to be hoped that other members of the community will respond to the student presence here and create affordable services for them, thereby enriching the diversity of the area. There is certainly no shortage of available space.

ADDRESS Gainsford Street, London SE1 [2F 79]
CLIENT London School of Economics
CONTRACT VALUE £5.3 million
SIZE 280 student rooms
TUBE Tower Hill – Circle and District Lines, walk over Tower Bridge
BUSES 42, 47, 78, 188, P11 to south side of Tower Bridge
ACCESS none

Bermondsey

Conran Roche 1987–1989

Bermondsey

Conran Roche 1987–1989

Camera Press

A very tight budget (£30 per square foot as opposed to a more usual £60) and a fast building schedule determined the design approach to what was once a 1960s' warehouse. It has been gracefully transformed into a photographic gallery on the ground floor with laboratories at the back, an open-plan office and meeting room on the first floor and a photographic library on the top mezzanine floor.

The two main features of the original structure, the concrete frame and the huge timber loading-bay doors, have been maintained but adapted to render a new character for the building. The most immediate requirement for the client was the creation of a warm, dry envelope. The concrete frame was stripped down to a skeletal state, then the side and rear elevations were infilled with Snowcem panels with stainless steel edging bands. The Queen Elizabeth Street elevation is glazed from floor to ceiling on the ground floor and the upper two storeys are infilled with untreated Iroko timber panels and glazing. The timber is an excellent insulator. Upper storey corner balconies hang out over the pavement, unsupported on the ground floor so that when viewed from Lafone Street the building collages itself onto the buildings behind rather than slicing them abruptly.

Internally, the architects have been equally creative but not preoccupied by limited resources. In the gallery, loading bay doors and fairfaced blockwork walls provide hanging space and the flooring is oak. Similarly, upstairs oak floors are the only lavish feature amongst an assortment of neatly detailed scaffold pipes as door handles, cheap building-site light fittings and another recycled door resting on shorter door sections becomes the boardroom table. The mezzanine floor is approached via an industrial spiral staircase and is accommodated within the height of the new profiled metal decking pitched roof. All services are contained within galvanised pipes and pinned to the concrete frame.

Panter Hudspith 1993

Bermondsey

Panter Hudspith 1993

The natural transformation of the external materials over time sets the building apart from other converted warehouses in that the approach does not try to ape urban industrial styles (inert white spaces with aluminium duct trim) but rather resembles a rural barn which responds to and is affected by the elements – the timber will gradually become bleached by the sun and each of the exterior concrete panels has the quality of blank canvas waiting to be painted by the rain.

ADDRESS 21/23 Queen Elizabeth Street, Butlers Wharf [2F 79]
CLIENT Camera Press
STRUCTURAL ENGINEER Cameron Taylor Bedford
CONTRACT VALUE £350,000
SIZE 990 square metres
TUBE Tower Hill – Circle and District Lines, walk over Tower Bridge
BUS 42, 47, 78, 188, P11 to south side of Tower Bridge
ACCESS to ground floor Tom Blau Gallery

Bermondsey

Panter Hudspith 1993

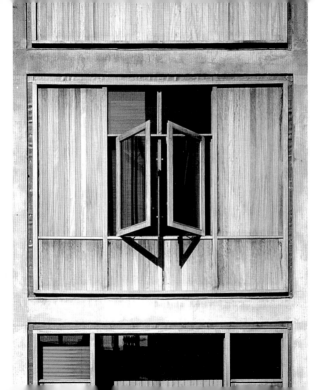

David Mellor Building

The David Mellor Building has been taken over by the Conran empire which domintes the area. It contrasts dramatically with the indigenous building stock as this project reflects the particular character of the original client. Mellor is to kitchen utensils what Terence Conran is to the rest of our homes. He had specific functions in mind for the spaces that were to be created, namely, a 3-metre-high glazed shop/showroom on the ground floor, with workshops and dimly glazed offices on the middle floors and a residence for himself high up on the top floor, in order to enjoy privacy and surrounding views of the dock.

Services are held in the gap between the main rectangular concrete frame of the building and Cinnamon Wharf on the north side. A solid, slate-grey stair tower is attached to the south side like the amputated limb of some much larger and more monstrous construction. The heavy slate effect is created by lead-wrapped panels hung onto the internal metal frame. Textured circular columns penetrate the glazed space on the ground floor. The materials used are not gleaming white and stainless steel as 1980s' kitchen etiquette dictates; the interesting way in which they have been used reflects an element of rural craftsmanship but on a factory scale (many of the items that were sold are made in Mellor's own factory in Derbyshire, also designed by Michael Hopkins). The Conran shop has had no trouble in adapting their look to the distinctive premises.

ADDRESS Shad Thames, London SE1 [2F 79]
CLIENT David Mellor
TUBE Tower Hill – Circle and District Lines, walk over Tower Bridge
BUSES 42, 47, 78, 188, P11 to south side of Tower Bridge
ACCESS to shop

Michael Hopkins & Partners 1990

Bermondsey

Michael Hopkins & Partners 1990

Horselydown Square

The scheme comprises four apartment buildings incorporating shops and two office buildings. The concept was the recreation of the character of traditional city planning by constructing a dense arrangement of buildings around two squares. At the centre of the main square is a fountain, designed by Tony Donaldson, surrounded by shops (most of them remain unlet so they have become makeshift galleries). The smaller square is cobbled, bringing together parts of the old city such as the Anchor Tap pub, and one of the new office blocks. The two squares are linked by a narrow passageway. The dense labyrinthine effect of the overall plan has also penetrated the design of the flats which spiral up to three storeys high, some with roof terraces or balconies and others culminating in turrets looking over into neighbouring streets. The exterior walls are rendered and painted terracotta and window frames are a brilliant blue.

All this sounds like you could be in the middle of an Italian hill town; however, the unlet shops and the distinct lack of domestic activity reeks of another quick shot in the arm for urban regeneration, all sewn up by providing a range of mixed-use buildings. You are offered office, retail and living space and the romance of Italy all done up in the same package. Rather like pre-packed sandwiches, whatever the filling, they all taste pretty much the same.

ADDRESS Horselydown Lane, London SE1 [17 79]
CLIENT Berkley House plc
CONTRACT VALUE £17 million
SIZE 14,200 square metres total
TUBE Tower Hill – Circle and District Lines, walk over Tower Bridge
BUS 42, 47, 78, P11 to south side of Tower Bridge
ACCESS to shops

Bermondsey

Wickham & Associates 1989

Bermondsey

Wickham & Associates 1989

The Circle

Approaching from either end of Queen Elizabeth Street, an unsuspecting visitor to the area will be ceremoniously engulfed in a vat of cobalt blue. Whilst deciphering whether one is in an interior or exterior space, tell-tale signs like the clouds above your head will indicate that this is simply a widening in the road. Appropriately industrial in scale, the glazed brick façades of this housing scheme form a circular courtyard (hence the name). The idea was to create more pavement in an area renowned for its unusual canyon streets – and a dropping-off point for cars, essential for the huge loads of shopping that residents amass from the out-of-town hypermarket, this being the only possible lifeline as retail units on the ground floor remain empty. The heavy cargo is then transported via one of two lifts in either the north or south lobby up to one of the seven storeys, along the corridor and into a conventional 1930s' prototype flat.

No decorative expense has been spared: diagonal glazing bars on painfully small windows and wavy brickwork parapets along street elevations. There is no disguising the fact that this project is simply a piece of superficial theatre. I half expected to be heckled by retired seamen from the bulky timber balconies that run diagonally up the façades, but there was no sign of such vibrant life. The Circle demonstrates that cosmetics are not enough to demonstrate or rethink a modern way of living.

ADDRESS Queen Elizabeth Street, London SE1 [2F 79]
CLIENT Jacob's Island plc
CONTRACT VALUE £32 million
SIZE 42,500 square metres floor space
TUBE Tower Hill – Circle and District Lines, walk over Tower Bridge
BUS 42, 47, 78, P11 to south side of Tower Bridge
ACCESS to shops

Bermondsey

CZWG Architects 1987–1989

CZWG Architects 1987–1989

China Wharf

This was CZWG's first big apartment building and it has become quite a landmark on the River Thames. Wedged in between two refurbished Victorian warehouses, it has three faces which reflect the types of industrial building in the area. One street façade is of London stock-brick, matching Reeds Wharf next door. The entrance courtyard façade has a scalloped face faintly echoing the scale and appearance of the industrial silos which once stood nearby. Windows are twisted towards the sun and away from neighbours. The scooped bottoms of each scallop, painted bright red, have provided superior lavatory facilities for the local birdlife. The river façade is more pagoda (owing something to its name) than Victorian London, its bold arches emphasizing the window type and then peeling off to provide visual support for balconies. The complicated interior is arranged on a scissor plan so that each flat has a view of the river and a private space at the back. The interior detailing is 1980s' kitsch, the exterior a Post-Modern cartoon.

ADDRESS Mill Street, London SE1 [2F 79]
CLIENT Jacob's Island plc; Harry Neal
Limited
STRUCTURAL ENGINEER Alan Baxter
Associates
CONTRACT VALUE £2.5 million
SIZE 1800 square metres
TUBE Tower Hill – Circle and District Lines,
walk over Tower Bridge
BUS 42, 47, 78, P11 to south side of
Tower Bridge
ACCESS none

Bermondsey

CZWG Architects 1988

Bermondsey

CZWG Architects 1988

Princes Tower

The building shows this particular practice's aversion to Post-Modernism by recalling the simplicity of form associated with the Modern Movement. Many influences are evident here, including Erich Mendelsohn's De La Warr Pavilion at Bexhill-on-Sea. Nautical motifs such as porthole windows and the cantilevered bay windows of each apartment overlook the river like the bow of a ship. The plans are greatly inspired by those of Le Corbusier; apartments have large open spaces, with a view of the river from the bath and stairs linking the parking space on the ground floor directly to each flat. The penthouse has the benefit of an observation tower and roof terrace.

It is remarkable that these riverside apartments were actually built in this style, rendered and painted white, in a conservation area where sprawling, low-rise, red brick Legoland-style developments are generally found to be sympathetic to their surroundings. The references to Modernist industrial design, part factory, part lighthouse, lend themselves to this riverside site, and the building acts as a look-out tower with its tiers of windows and radio mast on the roof.

The architects were not involved in the project beyond the design stage, so the quality of the final construction and detailing is poor. However, the scheme was received with open arms by the Royal Fine Art Commission and the Thirties Society.

ADDRESS Rotherhithe Street (near the church), London SE16 [2J 79]
SIZE 1200 square metres
TUBE Rotherhithe – East London Line
BUS 47 to Jamaica Road
ACCESS none

Bermondsey

Troughton McAslan 1990

Troughton McAslan 1990

Peckham Square

A project funded by the government's Urban Partnership Fund, this is part of a regeneration strategy giving a visible injection to blighted inner city areas. The scheme proposes a suitably flamboyant solution in the form of a marketplace, street theatre and general meeting place, beneath one roof. The 35-metre span of the canopy covers a raised and paved area (pattern designed by Alison Turnbull), sandwiched between boarded-up shop fronts from which its steel supporting members grow. Tension rods provide stability across the span. The roof area is covered in plywood and sealed with a waterproof membrane. Meanwhile, two circles are punched out to admit shafts of light and … torrents of rain, drenching the homeless people who have made it their roof and their space.

It is becoming increasingly evident that architecture is capable of taking on an even more dynamic role within the life of a city. A roof, in this instance, does not in fact fulfill its role as shelter, though perhaps it does as signpost, though to what is ambiguou. But it does act as scientific instrument. The architects worked with lighting designer Ron Haseldon to develop a 'meteorologically active' system – in other words, a barometer. Gels giving 16 colour variants illuminate the underside of the arch and change according to atmospheric conditions.

ADDRESS Peckham High Street, London SE15 [1G 95]
CLIENT London Borough of Southwark
STRUCTURAL ENGINEER Ove Arup & Partners
BR from London Bridge to Peckham Rye
ACCESS open

Bermondsey

Troughton McAslan 1994

Bermondsey

Troughton McAslan 1994

Docklands

Financial Times Print Works

From the 1920s until the 1980s, most of the UK's national newspapers resided in and around Fleet Street in celebrated office buildings which sat above basement printing works. The *Financial Times* was no exception and lived in Bracken House (designed by Sir Albert Richardson *c* 1959). However, with new editorial and production technology, it is no longer necessary for journalists, typesetters and printers to be together in the centre of the city, so in a positive gesture towards the regeneration of Docklands the FT moved to its print works within a year of its new home being commissioned.

The design of the building was determined by two printing presses which were already on order. This called for two 18-metre single-span spaces, one on the south side to accommodate offices and platemaking rooms and one on the north side to house the massive printing machines. These hall spaces run each side of a 12-metre-wide plant room. The full printing operation is on display through one big window (96 x 16 metres), following the tradition of this type of celebration of the printing process. The Pilkington Planar glazing system is made up of 2-metre square panes of 12 mm toughened glass bolted at each corner and sealed with silicone. The exterior fin-like steel columns, positioned every 6 metres, form a support for the roof and help to keep the glass in place. Positioning them on the outside of the structure leaves an uninterrupted internal space.

The structure of the printing presses dictates the organisation of the interior space, with four long levels, feeding rolls of pink paper from the bottom and pouring the ink from the top. The materials are stored and the finished product despatched (300,000 copies each night) in the two solid ends of the glorified shed. The skin is made from vacuum-formed panels of superform aluminium slotted together and resting on horizontal rails which collect rainwater away from the wall surface. Staircase towers

Nicholas Grimshaw and Partners Limited 1988

Nicholas Grimshaw and Partners Limited 1988

on the south side are also clad in aluminium, separating circulation from the office floor areas (fitted out by the Robinson Design Partnership).

Until now, the best time to see the print works has been at night between 21.30 and 2.30 (preferably by car because public transport is limited in this area) when the presses are running, but the latest news is that the building is up for sale. Contracts to print other papers have been lost and the plant cannot be justified if only the *FT* is being printed there. Any offers or suggestions for alternative uses are welcome.

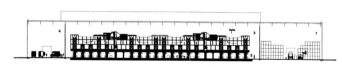

ADDRESS 240 East India Dock Road, London E14 [6C 64]
CLIENT The Financial Times
STRUCTURAL ENGINEER J Robinson & Son
DOCKLANDS LIGHT RAILWAY All Saints
BUS 5, 15, 15B, 40, 106, 277, D5, D6, D7 to East India Dock Road
ACCESS none

Docklands

Nicholas Grimshaw and Partners Limited 1988

Nicholas Grimshaw and Partners Limited 1988

Reuters Building

Another top-secret building in the Vauxhall Cross genre. This one houses the Reuters press agency. All of the information passing in and out of the building is electronic, invisible; hence the vast rooftop plant to control the internal environment which is primarily occupied by computers.

The black façade (like the tinted windows of a limousine) of the stumpy block is blind, allowing no visual access from the outside. Glazed stair towers are the only clue that humans inhabit the building. The small roof cranes and the partially unfinished quality of the roof plant (steel members are exposed where cladding has been left off) are undoubtedly the work of Rogers, emphasising, as much as possible, the operational aspect of the building rather than presenting an anonymous container.

ADDRESS Commodity Quay, East Smithfield, London E1 [7F 63]
CLIENT Rosehaugh Stanhope Development plc
CONTRACT VALUE £85 million
SIZE 27,900 square metres
DOCKLANDS LIGHT RAILWAY All Saints
BUS 5, 15, 40, 86, 106, 277, 278 to East India Dock Road
ACCESS none

Docklands

Richard Rogers Partnership 1989

Richard Rogers Partnership 1989

Storm-Water Pumping Station

The building houses a control and supply maintenance room for the electric pumps which are in chambers under the floor. When storm water flows from the Isle of Dogs into the underfloor chamber it is raised automatically into a concrete surge tank high above ground level and then forced by gravity into the Thames. The building is terrorist-proof and its concrete substructure is able to withstand an explosion. These factors explain why it is so massive in scale. Once you get over the sheer size of it and realise that the 3000-mm-diameter propeller does actually rotate at 16 rpm to evacuate gases that may build up inside, and appreciate the detailing that shows no signs of aging (after all it was built to last 100 years), you realise that you are looking at a windowless shed. It is also a monument, 'a temple for summer storms'.

Colours and materials link directly with the iconography: slate-blue bricks signify the river which flows through the two vast trees (columns) on the front and back façades, and red and yellow stripes signify the mountainside from which the water flows. The columns are not supporting the lightweight pediment but are disguising steps and ducts. Each element of the building has been embellished in a manner which portrays Outram's own imagination and fascination for assembling and exaggerating historical symbols.

ADDRESS Stewart Street, Isle of Dogs, London E1 [2E 80]
CLIENT London Docklands Development Corporation/Thames Water
STRUCTURAL ENGINEER Sir William Halcrow & Partners
CONTRACT VALUE £3.5 million
SIZE approximately 670 square metres
DOCKLANDS LIGHT RAILWAY South Quay
ACCESS none

Docklands

John Outram 1988

John Outram 1988

Jack Dash House: Isle of Dogs Neighbourhood Centre

Jack Dash House is the result of a collaboration between a developer, a borough council and a firm of architects who are more widely known for their refurbishment of West End clubs. It is unusual because it is a strong public building in an area which is a dishevelled monument to Thatcherite free-market economics. The building is named after the dockers' leader who died in 1989 but who had campaigned vigorously in his later life against the encroaching Canary Wharf development.

The plan is made up of three sides around a courtyard. The arterial west wing accommodates offices (highly insulated and naturally ventilated), the north wing contains a crèche which doubles as a theatre space and the south side forms the main entrance and linl; to the round tower which contains the Council Chamber and a gallery space below.

The costs of the building were kept very low by using the 'design-and-build method of construction, i.e. the architects design the building but the contractor is responsible for all construction. This means that detailing is often compromised. Despite this, the building stands out and represents a local council that has the flare to provide an imaginative working environment and a useful public space for the community.

ADDRESS Marsh Wall, London E14 [1C 80]
CLIENT London Docklands Development Corporation (for the London Borough of Tower Hamlets)
STRUCTURAL ENGINEER Price & Myers
CONTRACT VALUE £4.5 million
SIZE 4460 square metres
DOCKLANDS LIGHT RAILWAY South Quay
ACCESS open

Docklands

Chassay Architects 1990

Chassay Architects 1990

Pump House

This water-pumping station is part of the new infrastructure of the Royal Docks. It not only performs the essential function of lifting waste water up from underground channels to discharge into the River Thames, but It has also become a prominent landmark in the Docks. The design of the building was informed by its specific function. It was necessary to organise the servicing and operational requirements above ground in a low-maintenance, hard-wearing structure. This has manifested itself as two 12-metre-high concentric drums containing the electrical support functions. But this is just the tip of the iceberg. Inside there are 25-metre-deep shafts containing pumps and pipes. The surfaces of the concrete drums are brightly coloured and all steelwork is boldly detailed to maximise the impact of a building that is generally uninhabited.

With their vents and funnels, the pump houses in London are rather like elaborate tube-station entrances. Although there is no public access to the buildings, they are interesting to see just because they house machmes not people.

ADDRESS Tidal Basin Road, Royal Victoria Docks, London E16 [7H 65]
CLIENT London Docklands Development Corporation/Sir William Halcrow & Partners
STRUCTURAL ENGINEER Sir William Halcrow & Partners
SIZE 850 square metres
DOCKLANDS LIGHT RAILWAY Custom House
ACCESS none

Richard Rogers Partnership 1987–1988

Richard Rogers Partnership 1987–1988

Control Centre and Lifting Bridges

In the shadow of the monstrous Canary Wharf development, the gleaming Control Centre has invented an unselfconscious architecture all of its own. Deriving from the design intention to reveal all of the working parts of the bascule bridges, the architects have ingeniously created a separate building to house the hydraulic plant required to operate the counterweight system of the lifting bridges.

The simple steel-frame and steel-panel construction (welded on site) has been stretched and details exaggerated to create a bold, sculptural form. Each feature – gutter, air vents, staircase and control cabin – is an integral part of the structure, not a decorative afterthought. The great A-frames, pivots and hydraulic rams are now in full view, as are the mooring platform, fishing platform and public staircase – all dramatic silver elements set against the primary white structure of the bridges.

Many of these bascule bridges can be found in and around Chicago. This one, however, remains symbolic rather than practical as at present ocean liners do not navigate these docks.

ADDRESS Canary Wharf, Eastern Access, London E14 [80 E1]
CLIENT London Docklands Development Corporation
ENGINEER Mott MacDonald Civil Limited
COST £4 million
DOCKLANDS LIGHT RAILWAY Canary Wharf
ACCESS none

Docklands

Alsop Lyall & Störmer 1990

Alsop Lyall & Störmer 1990

Cascades

Twenty storeys high, with water on two sides, Cascades holds its head up defiantly in the middle of low-lying Docklands. From a distance the block seems to be a formidable solid lump with an unusual leaning profile, but close up it becomes multi-faceted, made up of layers of windows, balconies, turrets, and portholes. The texture of the façades is a result of the plan. A spinal corridor runs through the centre, either side of which are one-, two- and three-bedroom flats set at angles to capture interesting views and light. The flats have deep open plans with small cabin bedrooms tucked at the back (nearest the corridor). The sloping side is the fire-escape stair enclosed in a long shed-shaped enclosure (like a greenhouse) with roof terraces each side. The view is spectacular. Facilities in the development include a swimming pool (at the bottom of the slope), gymnasium, conference room and some shops.

It has been described as 'a castle for men and women of the right stuff', the types described in Tom Wolfe's novel, *Bonfire of the Vanities*. The block is a symbol of the 1980s' boom in finance and property. Young professionals as described above came to settle here. The site is convenient for getting to and from the City and was thought to be a good investment in the light of Canary Wharf, rising nearby. Now, many residents have become disillusioned as they are stranded in a location which still lacks basic amenities like a decent transport system.

ADDRESS West Ferry Road, London E14 [1C 80]
CLIENT Kentish Homes
CONTRACT VALUE £18.8 million
SIZE 164 flats
DOCKLANDS LIGHT RAILWAY South Quay
ACCESS none

CZWG Architects 1986–1988

CZWG Architects 1986–1988

Canary Wharf

Buildings and architects

1 Cabot Square – Pei, Cobb, Freed & Partners
10 Cabot Square – Skidmore, Owings & Merrill, Inc.
20 Cabot Square – Kohn Pederson Fox
25 Cabot Square – Skidmore, Owings & Merrill, Inc.
25 The North Colonnade – Troughton McAslan
30 The South Colonnade – Kohn Pederson Fox
1 Canada Square/Cabot Place/Docklands Light Railway Station – Cesar Pelli & Associates

The late Francis Tibbalds, writing in *The Architects' Journal* (7 November 1990), nicely summed up Europe's largest single development:
'If you want to see what, left to its own devices, the private sector produces, one need look no further than the Isle of Dogs in London's Docklands. The British Government's flagship of "enterprise culture development" and the urban design challenge of the century adds up to little more than market-led, opportunistic chaos – an architectural circus – with a sprinkling of Post-Modern gimmicks, frenzied construction of the megalumps of Canary Wharf and a fairground train to get you there. It is a disappointment to those who live and work there. Sadly, there was a necessary intermediate step between balance sheet and building that got missed in the rush. It is called urban design.'

Canary Wharf, excavated in the 1800s, is part of the Isle of Dogs. The warehouses were then the largest in Europe, some up to 1000 metres long. The port was abandoned at the beginning of the 1980s. At the same time, the Thatcher government set up the Urban Development Corporation to regenerate inner cities and to bring together the interests of business and

Skidmore, Owings & Merrill, Inc. (masterplanners) 1988–1991

Docklands

Skidmore, Owings & Merrill, Inc. (masterplanners) 1988–1991

property developers. The Isle of Dogs was declared an 'Enterprise Zone', to be monitored by the London Docklands Development Corporation. Emphasis shifted from creating places that would be accessible to, and that served the public, to market-led priorities; buildings for particular types of people, and especially for international business.

Canary Wharf was conceived as Britain's new financial centre, one of the three financial centres of the world, alongside New York and Tokyo. It was believed that the City's older buildings would not be able to cope with the demands of computerisation and a growing business population.

Canary Wharf was to have a new direct rail link directly to the City and its own airport connecting it to the rest of the world. It is precisely this lack of infrastructure that has been the downfall of Canary Wharf so far. An airport and rail link were built (by the LDDC) but the rail services have been poorly maintained and run sporadically. When you do reach the Isle of Dogs you face a grand canyon of office buildings although amenities are now slowly creeping in.

The site is long and thin with medium-height buildings of about 14 storeys around a central square. The plan claims to incorporate the patterns of London's Regency squares but there is little in either scale or proportion to substantiate this. The buildings are more 1930s Chicago in scale (most of the architects involved in the project are American firms).

The landmark is obviously the tower by Cesar Pelli. He describes it as 'a square prism with pyramidal top in the traditional form off the obelisk, which is the most archetypal way of creating a vertical architectural sign … this is the essence of the skyscraper'. It is the first skyscraper to be clad in stainless steel. Pelli used the material to symbolise the high-tech nature of the activities inside and to reflect what light there is falling on the building. He would have preferred the tower to be taller and more

Skidmore, Owings & Merrill, Inc. (masterplanners) 1988–1991

Skidmore, Owings & Merrill, Inc. (masterplanners) 1988–1991

slender, but the LDDC had already laid down rigid sizes for floor plans and heights. Five floors were consequently sliced off the top in order not to obstruct the nearby flight path.

The architects employed on Canary Wharf were really required to design façades for speculative office blocks, the size and shape of which had been predetermined, so the challenge for each one was to produce a sufficiently bland frontage to suit any occupant. The elevations and the interiors have separate logics. The result is variations on a theme: an international style of classical colonnades, single windows rather than bands of glass, and stripes of stone cladding.

It remains to be seen whether Canary Wharf will become a 21st-century metropolis. Perhaps the extension of the Jubilee Line will help to draw people to the site, but for the time being, with the prevailing economic climate, the development stands as a symbol of 1980s smash-and-grab culture.

ADDRESS Isle of Dogs, London E14 [D1 80]
DEVELOPER Olympia & York Canary Wharf Limited
CONTRACT VALUE approximately £750 million
SIZE 28.3 hectares
DOCKLANDS LIGHT RAILWAY Canary Wharf
BUS D5, P14 to Canary Wharf
ACCESS public spaces open

Docklands

Skidmore, Owings & Merrill, Inc. (masterplanners) 1988–1991

Skidmore, Owings & Merrill, Inc. (masterplanners) 1988–1991

Thames Barrier

The Visitors' Centre (for a nominal charge of £2.25, and the handbook at £2.95) will provide you with detailed information about the construction and the workings of the Thames Barrier in a typically early 1980s multi-media way, set to an equally suspect rock-opera soundtrack to heighten your experience of this genuinely remarkable engineering feat. The best bit is a model of the Barrier which actually rotates to demonstrate its actions at an intelligible scale.

The need for such a barrier arose from two main factors: the high-water level at London Bridge is rising by about 750 mm a century due to the melting of the polar ice caps; and the action of surge tides which originate as zones of atmospheric pressure off the coast of Canada. Where the warm Gulf Stream meets the cold Labrador Current the sea is raised approximately 300 mm. This hump of water moves across the Atlantic and occasionally northerly winds force it down the North Sea, sending millions of tonnes of extra water up the Thames.

Between 1953 and 1970 many schemes were proposed for different types and locations of barrages, guillotine gates and retractable bridges. One and a quarter million people spread over 116 square kilometres were at risk, so in 1970 the Greater London Council was given responsibility for the whole flood-prevention scheme. The width of the river is divided by piers to form six openings for shipping and four subsidiary non-navigation openings. Reinforced-concrete piers founded on coffer dams (watertight boxes of interlocking steel plates) support a rotating circular arm to which is fixed the silver moon-shaped gate. The seating for the gates is provided by concrete sills, containing service ducts, which were cast, then sunk to the level of the chalk riverbed. The largest sill measures 60 x 27 x 8.5 metres and weighs 10,000 tonnes.

The gates themselves – four of 1500 tonnes and two of 750 tonnes –

(Former) GLC Department of Architecture 1984

(Former) GLC Department of Architecture 1984

were manufactured at Darlington. These colossal elements had to be manoeuvred to within a maximum tolerance of 10 mm, fixed by divers working in zero visibility. The upturned hull-shaped roofs not only act as the symbolic feature of the Barrier above water level but also protect the operating machinery – reversible hydaulic rams that rotate the gates into any one of four positions. The roofs have timber shells covered with maintenance-free strips of stainless steel, which to this day gleam like medieval knights in shining armour.

Modestly referred to as 'the eighth wonder of the world', the Thames Barrier will protect London for at least another 30 years, taking a high estimate of rising sea levels. However, if there were a concerted international response to reduce the man-made causes of global warming, perhaps it would remain effective for even longer.

ADDRESS Unity Way, London SE18 [3B 82]
ENGINEER Rendel, Palmer & Tritton
CONTRACT VALUE approximately £500 million
BRITISH RAIL Charlton
ACCESS telephone 0181–854 1373 for Visitors' Centre opening hours and boat cruises

(Former) GLC Department of Architecture 1984

(Former) GLC Department of Architecture 1984

Docklands Light Railway, Beckton Extension

Ten new stations have sprung up along an 8-km stretch of land alongside Victoria Dock Road and the Royal Albert Dock Spine Road, extending the light-rail service to Beckton. Each uses a standard kit, designed to be both unified and flexible; to be identifiable as a route but able to accommodate different site conditions and station types, such as viaduct stations, island stations, stations built in the middle of roundabouts, and the terminus. Staircases, lighting, canopies and lifts have been designed on a modular system. Island stations (such as Prince Regent) and viaduct stations (such as Royal Albert) have cantilevered canopies supported by two sets of columns. A row of curved mullions extends from the main columns, spanning the tracks and then wrapped in a toughened glass skin. Electrical cabling is contained within the main columns. Lifts are the only coloured element (all other steelwork blending into the silvery grey dock-landscape), clad in red vitreous enamel panels, punctured by portholes on each level and glazed on the top to emit a beacon light at night.

The one fundamental flaw in the scheme was the primary consideration for the design of the whole project. Cost-cutting disguised as the Docklands Light Railway Streamlined Service of the Future means that the stations are unmanned – can a light, transparent structure alone accommodate all the safety requirements of passengers?

CLIENTS London Docklands Development Corporation, Docklands Light Railway
STRUCTURAL ENGINEER The Maunsell Group
CONTRACT VALUE £280 million
GETTING THERE the extension begins at Poplar Station
ACCESS open during train timetable hours

Docklands

Ahrends Burton & Koralek 1994

Ahrends Burton & Koralek 1994

Index

London: a guide to recent architecture

London: a guide to recent architecture

London: a guide to recent architecture

London: a guide to recent architecture

London: a guide to recent architecture

London: a guide to recent architecture

London: a guide to recent architecture

For photographs taken for this
edition, the publishers would like
to thank Stephen Dupont (pages 47,
125, 155, 193, 198, 199, 241,
277, 307) and Keith Collie (pages
65, 161, 163, 189, 190, 191,
201, 203)

Samantha Hardingham

London

This is the third edition of a book which *The Sunday Times* called 'the publishing hit of the season'. It describes and illustrates more than 100 projects, from shops and bars to the mega-developments in Docklands.

New entries include the first house built by Future Systems; community housing on the South Bank by Lifschutz Davidson; Troughton McAslan's flamboyant intervention in Peckham High Street, an attempt to inject energy into a blighted inner-city area; and the major infrastructure project extending the Docklands Light Railway to Beckton, with stations constructed from a kit of parts designed by Ahrends Burton & Koralek.

'... positively plump with exploring zeal and opinion ... Strongly recommended.' *The Observer*

Samantha Hardingham graduated from the Architectural Association School in 1993. She is the author of *England: a guide to recent architecture*, and a partner in a café in London.

ISBN 1-899858-08-3

9 781899 858088

THE TRIANGLE BOOKSHOP
Specialist Architectural Booksellers
36 Bedford Square, London WC1B 3EG Tel: 0171-631 1381

£ 5.95

970707=10<61287>HISHHARDJ/10646
HARDINGHAM S. LONDON-A GUIDE T

••• ellipsis KÖNEMANN